THE GREAT REVERSALS

THE
GREAT
REVERSALS

Tales of the Supreme Court

by Morris L. Ernst

WEYBRIGHT AND TALLEY | **NEW YORK**

Weybright and Talley
750 Third Avenue
New York, N.Y. 10017

Library of Congress Catalog
Card Number 73-76568

MANUFACTURED IN THE UNITED STATES OF
AMERICA

Contents

vi

Foreword

Law, as we have used it in our Republic, is a noble, subtle, and rare experiment of man. Out of about two hundred and twenty nations on our planet less than forty have ever pursued the search for truth—sometimes called justice—by adversary proceedings.

Out of 3⅓ billion total world population more than 1 billion persons over the age of fourteen years are illiterate in all languages. Only in the forty nations that have enough literacy to devise a system directed toward the choice of rulers do we find some form of court. Elsewhere there are rooms where tribal chieftains or other kinds of dictators hand down verdicts of guilt or innocence, right or wrong. A right of appeal from an unwelcomed decision is not yet within the imagination of millions of people on our planet. There is a handful of nations with literacy used as an instrument of dictatorship of the marketplace of thought as well as control over all disputes between citizen and dictator.

In slowly evolving cultures such as exist in scores of societies, law often maintains a pattern of rooted certainty. In a changing, that is a literate culture, certainty in terms of law—or life—is little more than an illusion. Even in a literate, changing world those mortals who have reached their pinnacle of success naturally desire to maintain the status quo that has been so kind to them. Particularly is this true of the majority of the so-called leaders of the bar. They who have done well under the old rules of behavior—called law—naturally do not care to run the risk of innovation or change. Thus the most prominent of our legal profession ran a violent, understandable campaign to prevent the confirmation of Louis Dembitz Brandeis as a justice of our high court.

I write this Foreword because, in my more than half century at the bar, I have always been intrigued at the entrancing dual objectives of law. Surely law must try to be precise enough so that our citizens shall not run the risk of guessing themselves into a lawsuit or jail, and still at the same time it must be subject to change so as to be meaningful in terms of the mores, the currently held beliefs of life, out of which judges must render verdicts acceptable to the people.

Judge Brandeis was one of the important mentors in my life. It was he who suggested to me the basic concepts of this volume. He left me his lamp from the Supreme Court bench, and while touching it I tried by osmosis to gain a bit of his wisdom and perspective, his insight into the reality that law changes with the changing conditions of life. Some of these changes are embodied in the stories of the Court's great reversals.

I have designed this volume not for lawyers but for the lay public. People are kept in ignorance about the law. In the main, the daily papers and the television programs manage legal events so that for most people law means only murder, mayhem, and divorce. I have tried to bridge the gap between the mystique of law and the vernacular of laymen.

Many of these reversals are historically more significant than the battles or earthquakes and catastrophes toward which our mass media are aimed. Part of the blame for such societal ignorance properly belongs to my beloved profession. Just as the ancient clerics tried to retain power by the use of Latin and just as the medicos even today write prescriptions in unintelligible gobbledygook, just so the big-city lawyers use a terminology that is unconsciously employed to maintain authority over the client seeking advice and comfort.

Hence, the great reversals of our Supreme Court have been unexplained by lawyers to clients, or by mass media to readers and viewers. And yet it is exciting to point to the need for legal change. We must keep in tune not only with plebiscites but with the pace of change within science and the other human arts. When the steamboat got itself invented, the law of the sailboat could scarcely apply. The law of trade unions had to be created by lawyers, and even today few lawyers or non-lawyers can with confidence predict what the law of the future should be in relation to the licensing of rainmakers, the lawful uses of artificial insemination, or the unidentifiable and unlocatable breaking of windows by, say, supersonic airplanes.

Surely not every first guess in these exciting avenues of human adjustment of desires between citizen and government, or citizen and citizen, can be ineluctably perfect.

In more than a hundred nations the subject of these pages would read like hieroglyphics. The forty-two Founding Fathers who sat out the four months of utterly secret debate in Philadelphia in 1787 and thus created our great Constitution never debated freedom of the "press"—a subject to be covered later in the great First Amendment to our Constitution. Little could they have foreseen movies, radio, television, or a communication satellite.

No other profession has the joyous duty of pursuing precision and at the same time keeping itself mindful of the need for change. The philosophy of the reversals of Supreme Court opinion shocks only those who do not understand the process or those who prefer to believe that law is handed down in buckram volumes from some judicial Mount Sinai.

The quality of life as lived in our culture and the rules of life called "law" depend upon the ability of the bar to communicate law to the laity. Of course, to our mass media, law means primarily, and often exclusively, murder, mayhem, and violence. But the fault—in terms of the gap between law and the citizen's knowledge thereof—may arise in part from the fact that the bar, like most professions, has its own proud vocabulary that is often unintelligible to laymen.

Hence I am proud that a non-lawyer has helped me on this volume. I am indebted to David Loth for his collaboration as a lay interpreter of law to non-lawyers in this narrative of how the Supreme Court rises above the virtue of small minds—consistency—to keep life and heart in that wonderful instrument of our national greatness, the Constitution.

MORRIS L. ERNST

THE GREAT REVERSALS

❧ 1 ❧

The Pace of Change:
1808-1810/1882-1967

Nothing reveals the Supreme Court quite so clearly as the way it changes its mind. This most powerful tribunal in the world has done it more than a hundred times since its first about-face in 1810, and it is always a traumatic experience for someone, usually the litigants and lawyers who relied on the old rule. One of the law's most revered maxims is *stare decisis*, meaning literally "to stand by decided matters." Upsetting it is never easy or frivolous. A look at the first and one of the most recent examples of the Supreme Court overruling itself may be a good introduction to the process and to unraveling a mystery of the judicial mind.

The first scene is the cramped, makeshift quarters in which the

Court was holding its session of 1808. The offices, borrowed until the Court's "permanent" home in the basement of the Capitol would be finished, were better than some—a tavern had to serve for one term. Only in the last few years had it attained the prestige of the most important state tribunals. In the beginning, many men were unwilling to accept a nomination. John Marshall twice refused a seat in 1798—Bushrod Washington, George's nephew, was finally appointed—and late in 1800 John Jay, who had been the first Chief, refused to return to that post because he did not believe the Federal courts were authorized to handle much serious business.

"The efforts repeatedly made to put the judicial department on a proper footing have proved fruitless," he informed President Adams. "I left the bench perfectly convinced that under a system so defective it would not obtain the energy, weight, and dignity which are essential to its affording due support to the national government, nor acquire the public confidence and respect which as the last resort of the justice of the nation it should possess."

On similar grounds, other early nominees preferred membership in a state legislature or a state court. One failed to appear even after he had been confirmed.

Fortunately for those who did consent to serve—the Court at this time consisted of a chief and six associate justices—they spent only six to eight weeks a year in Washington, still a muddy small town less than eight years old. They came without their families, traveling arduously overland by coach or horseback, the luckier ones being able to make part of the trip by coastal ship. While in the capital they lived together in the same boarding house, very much like a troupe of touring entertainers. They restricted their indulgence in alcohol to rainy days, but their Chief, John Marshall, had a way of reminding them, of an evening, that somewhere in the vast territory under their jurisdiction, recently doubled by the Louisiana Purchase, it must be raining, too. So, over a bottle, they continued their discussions of particularly knotty cases. Once they had decided, they would take quill pens in hand and write their opinions—in Marshall's Court it was usually the Chief himself.

At this point in its history, the overwhelmingly agrarian country consisted of seventeen states and an even larger national territory, much of it unexplored, which was administered by the Federal Government. This included all of the Louisiana Purchase plus the present states of Alabama, Mississippi, Indiana, Illinois, Michigan, and Wisconsin, the last still partly occupied by the British. The urban population was so badly outnumbered that Jefferson could survive his gibe that large cities add as much strength to a nation as running sores to a human body. The major non-agricultural industry was shipping, and this was at a standstill because of the war between England and France. An embargo imposed at President Jefferson's insistence had tied up 800,000 tons of seagoing vessels—most of the merchant fleet—and New Englanders (who owned the bulk of it) chanted bitterly:

> Our ships all in motion
> Once whitened the ocean,
> They sailed and returned with a cargo;
> Now doomed to decay
> They have fallen a prey
> To Jefferson, worms, and embargo.

Early in March 1808 the justices reviewed the exceedingly long and learned arguments that eminent counsel had been pouring out in *Rose v. Himely*. The case was one of several in which a difficult aspect of the Napoleonic wars, complicated by the struggle for Haitian independence, confronted the neutral United States. Small in population, five and a quarter million at the last census, the country had a rich shipping industry. The French had forbidden all trade with their rebellious black subjects, but American traders found the profits worth the risk. On February 23, 1804, less than two months after Haiti's declaration of independence, a French privateer seized the schooner *Sarah* with a cargo of coffee she had loaded at Port-au-Prince. The captor took her to a small Cuban port, Barracoa, and there, on March 18, sold the coffee to a Mr. Himely of South Carolina. When he got it home to Charleston, the original owner, Mr. Rose, sued in the Federal court to recover his property. He won, but the circuit court reversed the decision, holding that the United States had no authority to question the ruling of a French official in Cuba, "a person styling himself delegate of the French Government of Santo Domingo," the name the French still gave to the whole island. Rose appealed this judgment to the Supreme Court.

In those days, each justice also served as a circuit judge in the district where he lived. William Johnson was the member from South Carolina, and in Washington he held to the position he had taken in the circuit court, disclaiming power to examine or reverse the decision of a foreign tribunal. Chief Justice Marshall believed this far too narrow a view of United States authority. In his opinion, the Federal courts had a duty to review seizures on the high seas to determine whether they accorded with the law of nations. In this case, the law of war did not apply, he ruled. The United States did not recognize what he called "the brigands" who held Port-au-Prince and therefore must consider the island French territory subject to French "municipal law." If the privateer had captured the *Sarah* in the harbor, she would have been a legitimate prize. But she was at least thirty miles at sea, and so the seizure was "marine trespass." In Marshall's view, the *Sarah* was never under lawful French control, and no subsequent action by the "person" in Cuba or an even later hearing before a French court in the section of Santo Domingo still held for the Emperor could legitimize it. Rose should get his coffee back, and the circuit court should hear the case again to settle the costs each party must bear. Justice Johnson dissented.

Political issues in the Presidential year 1808, which became clear only after the Supreme Court session ended in March, were dominated by Jefferson's proposal to use a Treasury surplus (such things happened then) for roads and canals and by his maneuvers to keep the United States out of war. Increasing manufactures offset the slump in shipping so that the President wrote to Lafayette: "It has set us all on domestic manufactures and will, I verily believe, reduce our future demands on England fully one half." That year the first factory to make brushes opened in Massachusetts and Jesse Fell began to burn anthracite coal in Pennsylvania, while in the next two years the country saw its first silk mill, first ingrain carpet factory, and first screw factory. Political passions ran so high that anti-Jeffersonian shipowners talked of breaking up the Union. Timothy Dwight, Yale's clergyman president, preached to the text "Come out from among them be ye separate, saith the Lord." Out west in Kentucky, former Senator Humphrey Marshall, who had married the Chief Justice's sister, called the up-and-coming young Assemblyman Henry Clay a liar. In the resulting duel, the portly Marshall suffered a graze across his stomach and Clay a bullet in the fleshy part of his thigh. When James Madison was elected over Charles C. Pinckney by a margin of nearly 3 to 1 in the electoral college, the efforts to keep out of war and at the same time restore seaborne trade took new forms. This was the setting in which the Supreme Court overruled itself for the first time.

Another seized ship that had defied the French order was the *Sea Flower,* carrying coffee and log wood from Port-au-Prince to the Messrs. Hudson and Smith in the United States. She was taken by a French cruiser, also brought to Cuba, and sold under a judgment by a French court in Guadeloupe to a Mr. Guestier of Maryland. The United States court here found for Mr. Guestier in the first place, partly because the *Sea Flower* was captured within the territorial waters of a French island. When the district court reconsidered in the light of *Rose v. Himely*, it decided this made a difference and upheld its original finding for the purchaser. Hudson and Smith appealed, and in 1810 the case was back before the Supreme Court.

The world had changed more than the Court in two years—in fact, the same seven members still sat, although two of them missed this session. The central fact of life, even across an ocean, was the world war that had been raging intermittently in Europe since 1793 and was now grinding toward its climax. At the time of *Rose v. Himely*, President Jefferson had been trying to keep the United States out of it by prohibiting traffic with the belligerents. He hoped that loss of American supplies would force England particularly to allow neutrals the freedom of the seas and would end the impressment of sailors whom we called American citizens and she called British subjects. The embargo did not work. In 1810 President Madison was seeking peace through lesser measures that were leading to what contemporaries labeled "Mr. Madison's War" and the history books called the War of 1812. By now Americans were becoming painfully aware that belligerents respect no rights of neutrals or non-combatants whom they are strong enough to ignore. But hope lingered that Napoleon and King George might permit American ships to abide by American rules and regulations. Under the circumstances, the argument that no country should reverse the court judgments of another had a certain charm. Insistence that we might overrule the findings of a French tribunal was hardly compatible with our position that foreigners should respect our official findings.

As the five justices considered this situation, the arguments that had been so persuasive in 1808 lost their force. It must be assumed, the new logic ran, that the French hearing, wherever held, had considered all relevant argument and evidence, so the decision must be allowed to stand. The judges deliberately passed up a chance to rule in Guestier's favor without upsetting their *Rose* decision. The *Sea Flower* was said to have been captured in French territorial waters. Marshall in 1808 had suggested that here French "municipal law" would apply. But Justice Brockholst Livingston, who wrote the 1810 opinion of the Court, went out of his way to deal with this point, saying:

"I am not able to perceive how it can be material whether the capture were made within or beyond the jurisdictional limits of France; or in the exercise of a belligerent or municipal right. By a seizure on the high seas, she interfered with the jurisdiction of no other nation, the authority of each being there concurrent."

Presumably Justice Livingston's powers of perception had changed during the two years since *Rose*, for he had been with the majority then. The Chief Justice remained convinced that he was right in the first place, and in a brief, lone dissent he lamented his mistake in supposing that four colleagues had agreed with him in 1808. "The principle in that case is now overruled," he wrote. Justice Johnson, expressing satisfaction with the swing to his line of reasoning, explained in a concurring opinion that the course of events in the outside world was decisive:

"If I had no other reason to satisfy my mind of the correctness of the doctrines that I have been contending for, a conviction of their importance to the peace and security of the mercantile world would alone induce me to maintain them."

War is often a prod to men's thinking, as this example suggests. The more leisurely pace of change that is profound enough to cause the Supreme Court to overrule itself in time of peace is illustrated in one of the more recent examples. In 1967, the Court unanimously struck down a doctrine that it had unanimously upheld in 1882, and quite frankly explained that it was motivated by conditions that did not exist and philosophies unformulated in the nineteenth century.

Social changes in the lives of Americans between 1882 and 1967 reflected major physical changes. In 1882, the country got its first central electric station to supply light and power. Such things as long-distance telephones and paved roads outside the cities were unknown. Most people still lived in places with populations of less than 2,500 and without indoor plumbing. One out of five Americans was illiterate, as compared to one out of a hundred by 1967, and high school diplomas were as scarce in 1882 as college degrees at the later date. In no state in 1882 was a labor union legal or a trust illegal. The nation's population had gone from about 52 million to more than 198 million, and the voters in the nearest Presidential election from 9 million to 73 million.

The issues before the Court in both 1882 and 1967 were the institution of marriage, about which the justices rarely have to concern themselves on the bench, and the regulatory powers of the states, one of the problems that has always come before them frequently. They were asked to determine the constitutionality of laws forbidding blacks and whites to marry—the anti-miscegenation statutes. The case for upholding them had been stated by a Virginia jurist who took his law from the white man's heaven when the earthly variety failed his prejudices.

"Almighty God," he ruled, "created the races white, black, yellow, malay, and red, and he placed them on separate continents. And but for the interference with his arrangement there would be no cause for such marriages. The fact that he separated the races shows that he did not intend the races to mix."

This has the authentic ring of the post-Reconstruction South in 1882, but actually the judge was speaking in 1959, five years after the Supreme Court had handed down the most famous of its decisions outlawing racial discrimination. He did, however, have the authority of the 1882 decision to support him, and in more closely analogous circumstances, too. That opinion of the Court had been stated in no uncertain terms without any "separate but equal" rationalizations.

In November 1881, Tony Pace, a black man, and Mary J. Cox, a white woman, had been convicted in Alabama of the crime of "living together in a state of adultery or fornication." The judge had been lenient and sentenced them to the minimum penalty of two years in the penitentiary; he could have made it seven. The statute did not distinguish between mixed couples who were married and those who were not, because such unions were illegal in the state. Pace appealed the sentence on the ground that the law violated the Fourteenth Amendment's guarantee of equal protection of the laws. The Alabama penalty for adultery between members of the same race was only six months.

Justice Stephen Field, a Lincoln appointee who prided himself on being a rugged Californian—he had grown up in New England—delivered the opinion of a unanimous Supreme Court. He crushed the argument on behalf of Pace by pointing out that the six months section of the Alabama statute prescribed punishment for persons of different sexes while the two-to-seven years section established a penalty for persons of different races. The prison term for whites and blacks was the same under both clauses so both races had the equal protection of the law.

"There is in neither section any discrimination against either race," Justice Field assured Pace. ". . . whatever discrimination is made in the punishment prescribed in the two sections is directed against the offense designated and not against the person of any particular color or race."

This remained valid in most states, and seventeen still had anti-miscegenation laws when, in June 1958, Richard Loving, a white Virginian, went to the District of Columbia with Mildred Jeter, also a Virginian, but black, and married her. This was quite legal in the District of Columbia, but the couple soon went back home, and in October a Caroline County grand jury indicted them under a statute both more modern and more rigorous than the old Alabama model.

Racial barriers, far from lowering after the post-Reconstruction era, had increased the separation of the races. Although some blacks achieved status in scholarship, science, the professions, and even business, the principle of "separate but equal" became more and more the guidelines for race relationships, and all the emphasis was on the first word. Judge Lynch and Jim Crow were the chief authorities in the field through the last decade of the nineteenth century and the first of the twentieth.

They reached a peak in the 1920s, and the statute under which the Lovings were indicted stemmed from a Racial Integrity Act of 1924. This repeated the old prohibition against mixed marriages and stipulated that county clerks were to make sure applicants for licenses did not perpetrate any fraud. Also, any couple who went out of the state with intent to evade the law was to be considered as having violated it and to have incurred the penalty of one to five years in prison. The law defined "white" as "persons with no trace whatever of any blood other than Caucasian; but persons who have one-sixteenth or less of the blood of the American Indian and have no other non-Caucasian blood shall be deemed to be white persons." The registrar of the State Bureau of Vital Statistics explained this last clause as "the desire of all to recognize as an integral and honored part of the white race the descendants of John Rolfe and Pocahontas," several of whom were among the fabled First Families of Virginia.

From the highwater mark of such pronouncements as this Racial Integrity Act of 1924, the flood of prejudice began to ebb. The assumption of the absolute inferiority of the Negro on which much of the prejudice fed was exploded by science, and the doctrine of white supremacy was slowly discredited among large segments of the white population. After thirty years, when the Supreme Court marshaled the views of educators, sociologists, and other experts to upset public school segregation in 1954, the "separate but equal" dogma lost legal respectability, if not the support of the public at large. The Supreme Court, at least, had gone color-blind.

When they were tried in 1959, the Lovings pleaded guilty and their sentence of one year in prison was suspended on condition they leave the state and not return together for at least twenty-five years. From Washington, D.C., in November 1963, they asked a Virginia court to set that sentence aside on the ground that the

Racial Integrity Act denied them the equal protection of the law. Tony Pace had made the same plea in 1882. After some delays, the Virginia courts turned the Lovings down, the supreme court of appeals upholding the conviction on the basis of *Pace v. Alabama*, among other things. The Lovings appealed to the Supreme Court of the United States, where the case was argued in April 1967 in the stately palace that is such a contrast to the simpler quarters of Marshall's day.

Virginia held that *Pace* was still the law of the land, that neither Loving had been discriminated against because both got the same sentence. But this was countered to some extent by a much more recent ruling. While the Lovings had been waiting for the state courts to act, *McLaughlin* et al. *v. Florida* had been decided in 1964 and in the course of speaking for a unanimous Court, Justice Byron White had said:

"*Pace* represents a limited view of the Equal Protection Clause which has not withstood analysis in the subsequent decisions of this Court."

The Florida law under review set a penalty of a year in prison for a white and black of opposite sexes who habitually occupied the same room at night. This followed the section penalizing adultery between a white and a black more severely than the same offense between persons of the same race. The clause had been written because often it was difficult to prove the act of intercourse. Justice White pointed out that *McLaughlin* presented not quite the same problem as *Pace*. The *McLaughlin* penalty was clearly based on a color distinction, not an offense; it was not against the law for a man and woman of the same race to spend the night in the same room. Florida contended that the law was valid because it served the same purpose as the anti-miscegenation law. The Court dodged the question of that law's own validity, saying:

"We reject this argument without reaching the question of the state's prohibition against interracial marriage. . . . For even if we posit the constitutionality of the ban against the marriage of a

Negro and a white, it does not follow that the cohabitation law is not to be subject to independent examination under the Fourteenth Amendment."

Three years later in *Loving*, the Court could not longer avoid confronting *Pace* directly. Chief Justice Warren, who delivered the unanimous opinion this time, pointed out that the Virginia law was not as even-handed as its advocates maintained. It forbade only marriages between whites and members of other races, so even on its own terms it protected the "racial integrity" of no other ethnic group. But in any case, he went on, the discrimination on grounds of race was clear simply because race was the core of the so-called crime. Furthermore, the Chief Justice concluded, anti-miscegenation statutes violate another clause of the Fourteenth Amendment because they "deprive the citizen of liberty without due process of law." He explained:

"Under our Constitution, the freedom to marry, or not marry, a person of another race resides with the individual and cannot be infringed by the state. . . . These convictions must be reversed."

The two about-face maneuvers described in this chapter are fairly representative of the way the Supreme Court changes its mind, and the reasons that impel it to do so. The reluctance to overturn a precedent set by respected predecessors, the recognition of new conditions, the final plunge, often after several tentative rulings that do not quite reach the point of a reversal, are all typical. But the Court and the litigants before it have an inexhaustible supply of ingenuity in their approaches to the final step of actually overruling a previous decision. Any attempt to describe all these cases—a hundred or more—would be tedious as well as fruitless. No two authorities would draw up quite the same list. One thinks a given opinion overrules a former pronouncement. Another says the judges distinguished between the two cases. The remaining chapters of this book relate only examples that illustrate the law's ingenuity and at the same time

portray the role of the Supreme Court in an essential part of the
nation's development as Court and history reacted upon each
other.

An essential step in creating the public confidence and respect
that Jay had found so lamentably wanting was a retreat from the
judges' participation in party politics, such as had marked the
Court's first twelve years. All the justices belonged to the
Federalist Party until 1804, and in the administrations of
Washington and Adams they were looked upon as active partisans,
by themselves as well as by the public. Jay became the most
controversial figure of Washington's second term when he went
to England on a strictly political errand to negotiate a treaty that is
still known by his name. His successor, John Rutledge, had a recess
appointment from Washington but made such violent public
speeches against the treaty that when the Senate met after
Rutledge had presided over his only Supreme Court term, the
Federalist Senate refused to confirm him on a straight party vote.
The third Chief Justice, Oliver Ellsworth, harangued from the
bench against Jeffersonians as "apostles of anarchy, bloodshed, and
atheism."

All that came to an end after Jefferson was elected President and
the Federalists, it was said, "retired into the judiciary as remnants
of a beaten army into a fortress." With extremely rare exceptions,
they never emerged, and long before the Marshall Court had run
its course, the tradition of political aloofness was firmly established.
Since then, the politics that justices professed when they went on
the bench have faded into the more important background of their
fundamental political philosophy, although most of them were
deeply into politics when appointed. Marshall was Federalist
Secretary of State when he became Chief Justice (and thus held
two jobs for five weeks). Taney was Democratic Secretary of the
Treasury and had been Attorney General when he succeeded
Marshall. Although not a single Federalist remained, the twenty-
seven years of the Taney Court saw only three overrulings of its

Federalist predecessors, fewer than the Marshall Court's reversals of itself.

Mere whim, sudden or capricious fancy, also seem conspicuously absent. The judicial conference—that of the Supreme Court has yet to be violated by a leak, the presence of an outsider, or a tattle-tale participant—is not conducive to such vagaries. The notion that lightheadedness would strike at least five members at the same moment of deliberation is beyond belief.

The Court is seldom a mirror of the dominant social, economic, or political philosophy of the moment. Although it is more responsive to changing conditions than many of its historians have implied, it is sometimes behind and sometimes ahead of the nation's thinking. When a majority of the justices are conservative upholders of the status quo, the Court is slower to reverse a previous rule than popular opinion might be unless that rule itself overturned an older one. When a majority welcomes new ideas, the Court moves ahead of the national consensus.

The influence of Presidents who make the appointments and the politics that may surround confirmation is surprisingly slight. Nowhere in our governmental structure are conditions so favorable to complete independence as on the Supreme Court. The sole office of greater prestige, power, and dignity is the Presidency itself, and only one justice, Charles Evans Hughes, ever resigned to seek it. One other, William Howard Taft, who had been President, thought himself more fortunate to become Chief Justice. No Supreme Court member has been removed; the single impeachment trial, of Samuel Chase in 1804, resulted in acquittal on charges of gross political partisanship. A very few justices, becoming senile or enfeebled, have been quietly persuaded by their colleagues on the bench to retire; a striking example was Joseph McKenna in 1925 after his fellows agreed not to decide any case in which his was the deciding vote.

Presidents who presume that their nominees will follow the lead of the executive have been almost uniformly disappointed, and frequently enraged. Jefferson made all three of his appointments to the Court with the avowed purpose of getting a man to oppose John Marshall. All three concurred in a long line of opinions that angered Jeffersonians, and one, Joseph Story, became Marshall's devoted protégé. Lincoln selected a Chief Justice specifically to uphold two administration measures, only to have the man vote against the only one that got to the Supreme Court.

The Senate and public opinion have shared in maintaining this independence. Repeatedly the Senate has refused to confirm unqualified nominees despite the fact that the President's own party sometimes commanded a majority. In 1874, Grant proposed three candidates for Chief Justice, all described charitably by the biographer of the gentleman who finally got the job as "dubious." The President was forced to withdraw all three nominations because of public and senatorial clamor. Only once, and that a century ago, was a Supreme Court reversal accomplished by the simple expedient of appointing new members whose views were known on the issue, and that, too, was by Grant. Attempts to "pack the Court" have, with that single exception, failed conspicuously.

Lawyers who reach the haven of the Supreme Court, therefore, can indulge to the full their own concepts of what law and the Constitution command. They have no fear that a decision will prevent advancement, for they are already at the top. They are likely to be moved less by the opinions or exhortations of old associates, however greatly honored, than by their personal reactions to social change. They are, of course, moulded by their own experiences and studies within the framework of their individual natures and abilities. It is this combination that determines the direction they will take when confronted with the choice of affirming or rejecting the decision of a prior Supreme Court.

✎ 2 ✎

New Law for a New Country

At least three times after *Rose v. Himely*, the Marshall Court took an about-face on three different points of law. In all three of them the Chief Justice concurred, although he had written two of the overruled opinions himself. He also wrote one of the reversals. But before that, he got his hand in by reversing his predecessor, Oliver Ellsworth. The issue was nothing so portentous as war and peace or the freedom of a citizen to marry. The effects were mostly upon the work of the Court itself, fending off petty cases of no constitutional significance.

The need had arisen because the business of the Court, and its function in society, had outgrown the wildest imaginings of those who drafted the judiciary section of the Constitution, Ellsworth among them. They had supposed Supreme Court justices would spend most of their time riding circuit to handle the few local cases of Federal import. Sitting in the capital, they were expected to concern themselves with the disposition of a pirate ship seized at sea or a disputed boundary between states. The Marshall Court had changed all that. Good Jeffersonians thought it had usurped power that did not belong to it. Certainly it had more cases than Jeffersonians thought necessary.

In the years of the Marshall Court, most of its reversals were clearly triggered by a doubling of the national territory. From 888,811 square miles when he took office in 1801, the country had grown to 1,788,006; the acquisitions had cost just a little more than five cents an acre. Any rules that affected the disposition of this land had to have a profound effect upon the development of the nation, and the Supreme Court set some of the rules. Between 1800 and 1820, although population had increased from 5,300,000 to 9,600,000, the number of people per square mile had actually declined from 6.1 to 5.5. Furthermore, since the country would double again in size to its present 3,615,122 square miles, the early interpretations of land laws remain important. The preliminary patterns of Supreme Court changes of mind bear on this issue, too.

The precedent to be broken in 1828 was set in 1798 when William W. Wilson of Virginia appealed against a judgment for $1,800 that Thomas Daniel, an Englishman, had won against him in the United States circuit court. Daniel's lawyers asked the Supreme Court to refuse the case because the Judiciary Act limited the high court's jurisdiction over such cases to disputes involving more than $2,000. Wilson's counsel pointed out that Daniel originally asked for more and that that was what the statute meant. Ellsworth agreed, holding that Congress intended only that the original controversy involve more than $2,000, so the court award was irrelevant. Justice Iredell, who had been one of the judges who heard the case in Virginia, dissented and Justice Chase agreed only in part.

A very similar appeal came from Louisiana thirty years later. Francis B. Ogden had won a $400 judgment against Alexander Gordon for patent infringement, and Gordon wanted the Supreme Court to upset the award. He argued that Ogden had originally asked $2,600, and so "the matter in dispute" was enough under the 1798 precedent. Marshall, speaking for a unanimous Court, found little substance in the old rule. If the Supreme Court considered anything except the sum at stake when it got the case, everybody would always claim more than $2,000. He declared that "expense of litigation in this Court ought not to be incurred unless the matter in dispute exceeds two thousand dollars." He paid a compliment to his predecessor, which became itself a precedent for reversals, by trying to suggest that the wisdom of the earlier decision had already been eroded, so he was not bluntly contradicting Ellsworth. He explained that "we should be much inclined to adhere to the decision in *Wilson v. Daniel*, had not a contrary practice since prevailed." But in the cases he cited to illustrate this, more than $2,000 was still at stake when they reached the Supreme Court.

The next reversal was an early demonstration of the Court's deference to the will of the people. In two land title cases from Tennessee, the bench was asked to determine whether an act of the state legislature meant what it said or what the legislators and the people thought it intended. Since much the largest part of the nation's wealth was in real estate, and the process of settling even eastern states was far from complete, litigation over titles was a major preoccupation of the courts. The rights of a man who took up and improved land in the wilderness as against one who had a piece of paper but had done nothing about it until the other's toil made the place valuable were argued unceasingly. State and colonial laws designed to set the rules were seldom very clear, and one of the more ambiguous was a North Carolina act passed in 1715 when the future state still belonged to the heirs of the eight favorites to whom King Charles gave it in 1663. The law of 1715 was written for a province of perhaps six thousand people who had virtually no land communication with their neighbors. It had been held in its day both to confirm the man in possession after seven years of undisturbed occupancy, and also to evict him if someone came along with a grant of the same land given by the crown or a crown grantee. Later the state took the place of the crown. While Tennessee was still part of North Carolina, the state vested two hundred acres of what was to become the city of Nashville in trustees. They were to subdivide it and sell the lots, using the proceeds for specified civic works. In 1784, the trustees deeded a lot of Abednigo Llewellin, who had a son and heir fittingly named Shadrach. Shadrach sold the property in 1810 to Francis May, who promptly conveyed it to a man named Patton, who leased it to someone whose name never appeared in the court papers. Meanwhile, Josiah Love had taken possession of the land when Tennessee became a national territory after the War of Independence, and in 1793 he executed a deed for the lot to William T. Lewis, who made valuable improvements during the next seventeen years and in February 1810 sold to William Easton. Easton "continued peaceably possessed thereof," in the phrase of the final opinion, only until November when Patton's lessee brought suit to eject him.

The lessee claimed under the act of 1715, still valid when Abednigo Llewellin bought the land, and under a Tennessee law passed in 1797, the year after the state's admission to the union. The state law had been designed to protect bona fide settlers from grantees who never tried to take possession until the land became valuable. But, as Marshall said when the issue finally reached the Supreme Court in 1816, "As not infrequently happens, the explanatory law generated as many doubts as the law it was intended to explain." The most straightforward passage conferred title after "seven years' peaceable possession of any land, by virtue of a grant, or deed of conveyance founded upon a grant." While Easton argued that the law had been meant to protect settlers of seven years, no matter what, Marshall insisted—no doubt with some regret, for he had been raised on the frontier—that the words "founded upon a grant" could not be disregarded. Furthermore, he noted, Tennessee courts seemed to take the same view. Easton would have to go.

Sixteen years later, Asa Green found himself in exactly Easton's position, evicted from land he had occupied until another claimant's lessee came along to oust him. The district court in Tennessee applied the rule Marshall had stated in *Patton's Lessee v. Easton*. Green appealed to the Supreme Court to reverse itself. His lawyers pointed out that the Tennessee courts were now construing the 1797 law as meaning that possession for seven years transcended a grant. Not mentioned, but well understood by all, was the feeling of these Westerners against permitting their land to be taken from them by scraps of paper signed years ago in the East.

Justice McLean, for the Court, said that the justices always conformed their construction of state statutes to those of the state's own courts, and he cited a long list of opinions going back to the previous century. If the state's highest judges should change their rule in a series of adjudications, the Supreme Court would adopt the change for the same reason it accepted the earlier rule. "Especially in those respecting land titles," said Justice McLean, no state should be subjected to two conflicting laws of property, one its own and the other that of the Federal Government. So *Patton's Lessee v. Easton* was overruled, and Marshall concurred.

The about-face for which the great Chief Justice wrote both opinions also concerned titles to land, this time in Florida. A man named Foster had bought a tract between the Iberville and Perdido

Rivers in what for years Spain had considered West Florida and France had called Louisiana. The seller was a Spanish grantee who had received his document from the Spanish governor of Florida in 1804. When Foster came to claim his purchase after the United States bought Louisiana, he found one Neilson in possession, claiming title from the United States. The district court upheld Neilson on the ground that the United States had inherited France's claim to the territory, so that the grant Foster relied upon had been made by an "unauthorized person."

Foster appealed, and in 1829 Marshall gave the opinion of a unanimous Court that the district judge was right. He added that the treaty for the purchase of Florida, upon which Foster rested his argument for respecting the Spanish grants, provided only that such titles "shall be ratified and confirmed by an Act of Congress." Congress had never done this, so even if the French claim was invalid, the Spanish documents were worthless.

In 1831, the United States Land Commissioners in the new territory relied upon this last section of Marshall's opinion when they refused to allow Juan Percheman to take up a tract in what had been indisputably Spanish Florida. Percheman had an 1815 grant from the then governor, four years before the United States purchase. The district court interpreted the treaty as entitling Percheman to the land, and the commissioners appealed. Appearing for them in the Supreme Court in 1833 was the Attorney General, Roger B. Taney, the ardent Jacksonian who was to succeed Marshall, the only Chief Justice who ever received that post after the Senate had refused to confirm him as an associate justice.

U.S. v. Percheman, as presented to the Court, contained one element that had not been present in *Foster v. Neilson*. The defendant had a Spanish copy of the treaty, and that said the old regime's grants "shall remain ratified and confirmed." The Chief Justice pointed out that the slight difference in phrasing made all the difference. The Spanish text did not indicate that legislation was needed to impose a binding obligation upon the United States, as did the English version. Marshall explained that at the time of *Foster* the Court assumed the two versions were identical. "The Spanish part of the treaty was not then brought to our view," he said. "Had this circumstance been known, we believe it would have produced the construction we now give to the article."

These three turnabouts were in a sense prologue to a more important change of opinion. This one had to wait both for Marshall's successor and for judicial recognition that the vast size of the country demanded alterations in economic and legal concepts. In the development of the continent, transportation has played such a key role that each new medium for moving goods and people has accomplished its own revolution. The first was the steamboat. It both facilitated and complicated the use of America's network of inland rivers and lakes. But the full consequences were hardly predictable in 1825 when the case of *The Steam-Boat Thomas Jefferson, Johnson and Others, Claimants*, came before the Supreme Court.

For several years, the Court had been accommodated in quarters of its own, rather small, in the basement of the Capitol beneath the Senate. A long table and arm chairs on rollers were set out for the bar. A few seats for spectators were provided, but most stood among the arches that held up the Senate floor and gave the impression, according to one Senator, of "the prison of Constance in Marmion." But people did come and stand, because the oratory of counsel, addressing the justices on their slightly raised platform, was one of the fashionable entertainments of a capital that was shy of most of the other performing arts. Favorites, such as Daniel Webster, played to the gallery and sometimes kept a single speech going for three days.

The Thomas Jefferson inspired no such eloquence. The legal problem it raised was the extent of the admiralty jurisdiction of the Federal courts. Water transportation on a large scale produces a great many disputes between shippers and carriers, crews and owners, passengers and agents, competing ships and colliding ships. Under the rule that the United States had inherited from England, admiralty courts heard cases arising from incidents on the open ocean or tidal waters. Anything that happened on lakes or rivers beyond the reach of the tide was for the ordinary courts. In the United States, these would be state courts almost always because the waters were state territory. But admiralty rules have certain technical advantages for some litigants. In the matter of *The Thomas Jefferson*, the advantage to Johnson and "Others" was that they could "libel" or seize the ship to satisfy their claim, which was for wages (disputed by the employer) earned on a voyage from Shippingport, Kentucky, up the Missouri River and back again.

The shipowners pointed out that the nearest tidewater was a thousand miles away or more, so the United States courts could have no jurisdiction. The Court agreed. Justice Joseph Story, one of the most eminent of American judges and an admiralty authority, gave the unanimous opinion that jurisdiction of Federal courts over inland waters ended where the ebb and flow of the tide stopped. He wrote a similar opinion in 1837 after Taney had succeeded Marshall. In the 1825 decision, he hinted broadly that Congress could remove any serious difficulties his ruling caused if it so desired.

"Whether, under the power to regulate commerce between the states, Congress may not extend the remedy, by the summary process of the Admiralty, to the case of voyages in the western waters, it is unnecessary for us to consider," he said. "If the public inconvenience, from the want of a process of an analogous nature, shall be extensively felt, the attention of the Legislature will doubtless be drawn to the subjects."

The public inconvenience was so great in the next couple of decades that in 1845 Congress adopted Story's suggestion and based extension of Federal jurisdiction over inland waters on the interstate commerce clause. But a good deal of the commerce on lakes and rivers was not interstate, and what happened then? The answer to that question became increasingly important as the American tide of empire flowed west to Texas and on to the Pacific coast. New cities developed into great ports hundreds of miles from the sea, and commercial disputes expanded as rapidly as the commerce itself. When Story spoke in 1825, Louisiana and Missouri were the only states west of the Mississippi, and the old Northwest Territory was still so empty that neither Wisconsin nor Michigan warranted statehood. By 1850, both of these were states and so were Arkansas, California, Texas, and Iowa. Ships on the Mississippi were as luxurious and nearly as big as any on the ocean. Much of the traffic, however, continued to be within the boundaries of a single state.

In 1825, the first steam tug, the testing of the first iron ship, and the opening of the Erie Canal were a few indications that a new era of inland transportation was about to begin in the opening of the West. Before the Erie Canal, the whole Great Lakes region was commercially inaccessible. The cost of transporting grain from there to New York City was from three to twelve times the value of the produce. The Canal reduced freight rates to less than 10 percent of the old charges. As yet no railroad operated commercially, although in 1824 John Stevens built a locomotive that would pull a car around a circular track on his Hoboken estate. The first highway to be built with Federal funds, from Cumberland, Maryland, to Vandalia, Illinois, was about half finished.

By 1851, the Federal commitment to transportation was well established. That year ground was broken for the Illinois Central, the first railroad to receive a substantial Federal land grant, 2,500,000 acres. This was also the year that the first railroad west of the Mississippi was started and, foreshadowing a much later development, the Baltimore and Ohio ran an electric locomotive powered by storage batteries for a ten-mile round trip from Washington to Bladensburg, Maryland, at a speed on one stretch of nineteen miles an hour.

The incident that led the Court to reverse Story's opinion about the admiralty role of Federal courts took place on a calm, clear night in May 1847, when the steamship *Genesee Chief* ran down and sank the schooner *Cuba* on Lake Ontario. In spite of the fact that the collision took place in New York territorial waters and all concerned were citizens of New York, the *Cuba's* owners chose to libel the steamship in Federal court, and won a verdict. In due course, the appeal came up to the Supreme Court under the resounding title: *The Propeller Genesee Chief, Her Tackle, Apparel, and Furniture, William L. Pierce, Master, Alexander Kelsey, William H. Cheney, William Hunter, Lansing B. Swan, George B. Swan, George R. Clark, and Elisha D. Strong, Appellants v. Henry Fitzhugh, Dewitt C. Littlejohn, and James Peck.* The law books understandably refer to it simply as *The Genesee Chief*.

The appellants' argument was that the law of 1845 was unconstitutional because it did not attempt to regulate interstate commerce, just extended the jurisdiction of the Federal courts into an area from which the Constitution barred them. For the Constitution defined the judicial power of the United States as covering "all cases of admiralty and maritime jurisdiction," and that meant only on the high seas or in tidal waters. The owners of the *Cuba* pinned their faith on the commerce clause.

Chief Justice Taney brushed both these arguments aside when he delivered his opinion in 1851. He was a strange mixture of slave-owner, aristocrat, and Jacksonian democrat, clinging to the past but conceding the need to accept the future. He introduced the custom of judges wearing trousers under their robes instead of the more formal knee breeches. On principle, he was not inclined to stretch the commerce clause to anything like its later elasticity. He did not believe it justified the law of 1845. But he rejected the appellants' argument, too. He said, speaking for a majority of the justices, that the grant of judicial power to Federal courts was quite wide enough because all navigable waters "are within the scope of admiralty jurisdiction as known and understood in the United

States when the Constitution was adopted." He did not attempt to gloss over his certainty that the Court had been wrong in its *Thomas Jefferson* decision. He explained the about-face as necessitated by economic changes that were completely incompatible with the old English rule, made for a country that had no navigable inland waters.

"The conviction that this definition of admiralty powers was narrower than the Constitution contemplated," he said, "has been growing stronger every day with the growing commerce on the lakes and navigable rivers of the western states."

Later in his opinion, he explained why he and his colleagues felt justified in overruling the Story opinion, saying:

> It is the decision in the case of *The Thomas Jefferson* which mainly embarrasses the Court in the present inquiry. We are sensible of the great weight to which it is entitled. But at the same time, we are convinced that, if we follow it, we follow an erroneous decision into which the Court fell, when the great importance of the question as it now presents itself could not be foreseen . . . For the decision was made in 1825, when the commerce on the rivers of the west and on the lakes was in its infancy, and of little importance, and but little-regarded compared with that of the present day.
>
> The case of *The Thomas Jefferson* did not decide any question of property . . . And as we are convinced that the former decision was founded in error, and that the error, if not corrected, must produce serious public as well as private inconvenience and loss, it becomes our duty not to perpetuate it.

The Court has never called a predecessor mistaken in blunter language. Later justices might not have been quite so blatant in their assumption that property is better entitled to protection than wages, and some would not even have agreed with that point of view. But it would be a long time before the priority of property would be overthrown.

It was not on such grounds that Taney failed to carry the full Court with him. Justice Daniel, although much less inclined than the Chief Justice to be bound by precedent, dissented. He thought "admiralty" still meant what the English said. He also disliked any extension of Washington's power over people or the economy. The excuse that national expansion and growth demanded increasing central authority had small appeal to him.

"My opinions," he said, "may be deemed to be contracted and antiquated, unsuited to the day in which we live; but they are founded upon deliberate conviction as to the nature and objects of limited government, and by myself at least cannot be disregarded; and I have at least the consolation—no small one, it must be admitted—of the support of Marshall, Kent, and Story in any error I may have committed."

While Taney was pleased not to have upset a precedent involving property, the history of his long tenure as Chief Justice—only Marshall served longer—suggests that he would have been flexible enough to find another reason for overruling *The Thomas Jefferson* even if he had had to find the law of 1845 constitutional. The main point, after all, was to permit the Federal judiciary to facilitate rather than hamper the growth of commerce and the settlement of the vast new territories acquired in the first half of the century. Taney already had proved that he was quite capable of reversing the Marshall Court even when property was at stake.

3

The Emancipation of Corporations

The circumstances that led to the other important about-face of the Court under Taney were as significant for the country's development as the opening of the West, and contributed in some measure to the way in which the West was opened. United States corporations have played their enormous role in the American economy along the lines they did partly because a doctrine stated in 1806 and confirmed in 1809 was overruled in 1844.

Corporations as creatures chartered by the state were familiar enough, but up to this period in United States history they had seldom been large enough or ambitious enough to carry on much business outside of the state of incorporation. Problems arose when corporations began to replace partnerships and individuals in nationwide commercial ventures and took over large areas of banking, insurance, and transportation across state lines. A recurring question before the Supreme Court was the legal status of corporations in the Federal courts for purposes of suing and being sued. The simple solution—that a corporation is just like a citizen in this respect—was unacceptable to most people. A large proportion, perhaps a majority, thought these chartered bodies already had too great privileges and immunities without adding those of citizenship. Since most monopolies were vested in corporations, some people regarded all corporations as monopolies. Suspicion of banks and speculators, a cardinal tenet of popular parties from Jefferson to Jackson, heightened the distaste for conceding anything to joint stock companies.

The Supreme Court had its first crack at this tough corporation nut when *Strawbridge v. Curtiss* turned up on the docket of 1806. At this stage of our jurisprudence, the suit had to be brought in the name of all the human members of one corporation against all those of another. The United States circuit court in Massachusetts had dismissed a bill in chancery brought by the Strawbridge group, a corporation, against the Curtiss group, also a corporation. The court said it had no jurisdiction because all the parties were citizens of Massachusetts except Curtiss, who hailed from Vermont. This exception was not enough, the district judge ruled, to give the case that "diversity of citizenship" needed to bring a dispute into the United States courts. Whereupon the issue was submitted to the Supreme Court, without argument, solely to determine jurisdiction.

Marshall, who wrote for the Court as he usually did, quoted the act of Congress that delimited the types of cases to be heard in Federal courts: "where an alien is a party; or the suit is between a citizen of a state where the suit is brought and a citizen of another state." This meant, the Chief Justice decided, that every one of the plaintiffs must be able to sue every one of the defendants. While all of the Strawbridge contingent could sue Curtiss in a Federal court, they could not sue any of the Vermonter's co-members of the corporation. Furthermore, if a Vermonter had been among the Strawbridge group, their corporation would have been barred from suing Curtiss. Marshall made it clear that the ruling applied only to people banded together in a corporation. He pointedly refrained from offering an opinion "where several parties represent several distinct interests."

Marshall reaffirmed this principle and was even more precise about the legal status of corporations when in 1809 he gave the Court's opinion in *Bank of U.S. v. Deveaux* et al., which came up from Georgia. That state in 1805 had passed a law levying a tax on the Savannah branch of the Bank of the United States, the Hamiltonian institution that was anathema to all good Jeffersonians. (This issue would evoke a much more important Marshall opinion in 1819, *McCullough v. Maryland*, denying a state's authority to tax Federal agencies.) The bank refused to pay and, on April 20, 1807, Peter Deveaux, a state official, sent agents into the bank's offices. They, in the words of the bank's petition for redress,

> with force and arms entered into the house and premises of your petitioners . . . and then and there seized, took, and detained, two boxes (the goods and chattels of your petitioners) containing each one thousand dollars in silver . . . and carried the same away, and converted and disposed thereof to their own use, and other wrongs to your petitioners then and there did against the peace of the district, and to the great damage of your petitioners, and therefore your petitioners say they are injured, and have sustained damages to the value of three thousand dollars.

The petitioners made another point. They "averred" that they (the corporators of the Bank of the United States) were all citizens of Pennsylvania, where the bank had its headquarters, and the defendants were all citizens of Georgia. ("Aver" was used here to convey more certainty than "allege," but avoided committing the bank to "swear.") The lower court had held that the bank could not, as a corporation, be a citizen of anything, and so had declined jurisdiction.

This case was argued at length by two of the most popular orators at the Supreme Court bar, Philip Barton Key, whose brother was later the author of "The Star-Spangled Banner," and Robert Goodloe Harper, a favorite of the Federalists, who appeared on behalf of the bank. Both were masters of the art, so much admired in their day, of saying the same thing over and over again in different and more flowery language each time. They were among the pleaders who led Marshall to exclaim one day when told that he had reached the acme of judicial distinction: "Hah! You know what that means? It means the ability to look a lawyer in the eye for an hour and not hear a damn word he says." On this occasion, both Key and Harper strayed far afield to embellish their arguments with what the audience considered many pleasing metaphors.

Key, for the Georgians, went into a long explanation of why a corporation could not possibly be a citizen. It had no organs but a seal. It could not die or appear in person or commit treason or a felony. Finally, he exclaimed triumphantly, this artificial, invisible body, existing only in the law's mind's eye, could not be a citizen because it could not take an oath of allegiance.

Harper's reply was that a corporation was like a woman—lawyers then argued ingeniously that a woman could not be a citizen because the word can apply only to males. Incorporation, said Harper, is a privilege people acquire without losing any rights they already have, such as suing, just as a woman acquired the privilege of being free from arrest for debt when she married, but did not lose the privilege of inheriting land. He made the more pertinent claim that the bank had a right to bring this case in the

Federal courts because its charter said it could sue and be sued, a common phrase in such documents.

Marshall disposed of that argument first. A charter, even one granted by Congress and signed by the President as this one had been, conferred no right to sue where an individual in the same circumstances could not. Then, he pointed out, the Federal courts were for suits "between citizens of different states." Up to a point Marshall agreed with Key, saying:

"That invisible, intangible, and artificial being, that mere legal entity, a corporation aggregate, is certainly not a citizen, and consequently, cannot sue or be sued in the courts of the United States . . ." But the Chief Justice was not ready to place corporations completely outside the law, so he added ". . . unless the rights of the members, in this respect, can be exercised in their corporate name."

So the members—often the phrase used was "the president, directors, and company" of such-and-such corporation—could come or be brought into court. But if it was a Federal court, they had to be citizens of a different state, every one, than all the parties on the other side. In this case, the "averment" that all the bank's members were citizens of Pennsylvania entitled them to sue Georgians in the United States district court. Therefore, the judgment of that court was reversed, and the principle of *Curtiss* strengthened. No one seems to have brought up the point that the "averment" was a barefaced lie. The twenty-five thousand shares of the first Bank of the United States were widely held and in many states.

The consequences of these decisions were not immediately felt very strongly, because only a few banks and insurance companies had stockholders in several states. But those that did found themselves able to avoid being taken into a Federal court when they preferred to settle a dispute in their home state, where they usually had more influence over a judge than they did elsewhere. Or, if they wished to sue someone else in that person's home state, they could go to Federal court by the device of "averment" and avoid an unfriendly local judge.

When Marshall wrote his opinion in 1806, corporations were so unusual in business that each had to be chartered by a separate act of a legislature. Then in 1811 New York authorized its Secretary of State to issue charters and the rush was on. Commercial banks had been unknown in the colonies; the first dated to 1781 when Robert Morris incorporated the Bank of North America. Only twenty-nine chartered banks existed in 1800, fewer than fifty in 1806, and the country had its first bank failure in 1809. Hundreds of banks had incorporated by 1845, down somewhat from an estimated seven hundred before the depression of 1837–44 ruined many. Insurance went further back than banking, but the first corporation in the field, the Insurance Company of North America, was formed in 1792 in Philadelphia, where the first life insurance company was organized in 1809. By the middle 1840s, life insurance was operating along the present lines. Of course, no railroad companies existed in 1806; the first, the Baltimore and Ohio, dates to 1827. But by 1845 dozens had been incorporated—many were no more than paper—and twenty of the real ones chartered at that time still survive. It was estimated that some four thousand miles of track were carrying freight and passengers. Trading and manufacturing corporations were rare in 1806, most businessmen preferring partnerships if they were not loners. By 1845, the corporation was becoming a favorite form of organization for all kinds of business, especially in New England.

As the operations of large corporations expanded, the Marshall rulings became increasingly obnoxious to a great many litigants, most of them businessmen of considerable repute. Judges began to have doubts as to the soundness of Marshall's reasoning, and he himself was understood by his colleagues to regret the decisions. Yet such was the force of the precedent that the Supreme Court upheld his rule even five years after he died in 1835.

Its 1840 affirmation resulted from an attempt by the trading firm of Slocombe, Richards, and Co. of Louisiana to collect on a certificate of deposit from the Commercial and Rail Road Bank of Vicksburg. In those days of very lax regulation of banking and the carefree spirit in which many bankers used other people's money, it was often much easier to make a deposit than a withdrawal. Local courts were especially cavalier about enforcing claims of depositors from another state, especially if the bank had taken care to have a few official friends. This bank tried to remove the issue from the United States district court for Mississippi on the ground that two bank stockholders were citizens of Louisiana. The judge dismissed this plea as irrelevant in spite of *Curtiss* and *Deveaux*. In the ensuing trial, Slocombe, Richards won a verdict of $3,541.34. The bank appealed, and through Justice Barbour, the Supreme Court upset the award solely on the strength of the old Marshall decisions.

Soon another district judge, this one in North Carolina, refused to be bound by *stare decisis*. The Louisville, Cincinnati, and Charleston RR. Co., with headquarters in North Carolina, asked him to refuse to hear the case of Thomas W. Letson, a New York contractor who was trying to collect for helping to build the railroad. The company said not all its stockholders lived in North Carolina, and that in fact some banks and insurance companies that owned stock in the railroad had stockholders of their own who were residents of New York. The judge said this made no difference, regardless of what the Supreme Court had said, and decided that the company owed Letson $18,140.23. The loser appealed, strictly on the basis of the unbroken precedents of *Curtiss*, *Deveaux*, and *Slocombe*, and in the 1844 term the Supreme Court listened to a rehash of the old arguments.

Although all three of the previous cases had been decided by unanimous vote of the Court, the justices now were in agreement that the rule must be abandoned. Justice Wayne, after reviewing with compliments the brilliant debate of counsel in *Deveaux*, paid tribute to the ability of the lawyers he had heard.

And now [he went on], we are called upon in the most imposing way to give our best judgment to the subject, yielding to decided cases everything that can be claimed for them on the score of authority except the surrender of conscience.

After mature deliberation, we feel free to say that the cases of Strawbridge and Curtiss and that of the Bank and Deveaux were carried too far. . . . We do not think either of them maintainable upon the true principles of interpretation of the Constitution and the laws of the United States. . . . We remark, too, that the cases . . . have never been satisfactory to the bar, and that they were not, especially the last, entirely satisfactory to the Court that made them. They have been followed always most reluctantly and with dissatisfaction. By no one was the correctness of them more questioned than by the late Chief Justice who gave them. It is within the knowledge of several of us that he repeatedly expressed regret that those decisions had been made.

Then, after noting that the Court's 1840 opinion "was most reluctantly given upon mere authority," Justice James Wayne announced that he and his colleagues rested their present judgment upon much broader ground than had been previously considered.

It is [he explained], that a corporation created by and doing business in a particular state, is to be deemed to all intents and purposes as a person, although an artificial person, an inhabitant of the same state, for the purposes of its incorporation, capable of being treated as a citizen of that state, as much as a natural person. Like a citizen it makes contracts, and . . . it is substantially, within the meaning of the law, a citizen of the state which created it, and where the business is done, for all the purposes of suing and being sued.

Just as his Chief, Taney, was to do in *The Genesee Chief*, Wayne rejoiced that the Court's departure from the Marshall decision "involves no change in a rule of property." He also ventured the opinion that even those who opposed the Court's present ruling would admit it to be "coincident with the policy of the Constitution and the condition of the country."

4

A Precedent for Reversals

Even in the first decade of the Taney Court, Story and Webster, among many, mourned what they considered the utter decay of the Federal judiciary through a servile pandering to leveling principles of Jacksonianism and weakening of the safeguards of property. Story even deplored the increase to nine justices for the 1838 term, a recognition of the greatly expanded size of the territory they served as circuit judges. He complained that too much time went into procedure and too little into work. With twelve judges, he commented, the Court would get nothing done at all.

From the vantage point of today, the outcry seems fearfully

exaggerated. Taney was as dedicated to property rights as Marshall, although he emphasized slaves and land rather than contracts. He did modify the more extreme interpretations that men attempted to read into Marshall's nationalist opinions, for the new Chief Justice was a strong states' rights man. But, like the greatest states' rights philosopher, Jefferson, he was quite willing to use Federal power for ends he approved. In the long run, therefore, the Taney Court, which spanned more years than any other except Marshall's, overruled itself as often as it overruled its predecessor.

Most of the cases in which this occurred, as most of the work of the Court, involved no fundamental, disputed construction of the Constitution. The vast bulk of litigation that rises to this level of adjudication concerns the interpretation of lesser documents— sections of a statute, rules of procedure, the intent of legislators. But to the litigants who gain or lose liberty or property as a result of the decision, the ruling is as important as if it construed the fundamental law itself. The opinion may be equally important in the future, although legislatures find it easier to change the basis for the decision than to change the Constitution. So any Supreme Court pronouncement can have profound repercussions for many years to come.

During the decades before the Civil War, the Court demonstrated two patterns of self-reversal that in themselves may almost be considered precedents—precedents for an about-face—although these were not always brought about by economic or social development or new discoveries in science and technology. The change was at times in the attitudes of the justices themselves.

At times, these eminent jurists concluded that their predecessors or they themselves had been mistaken. When they could not reach what they now considered a correct decision by "distinguishing" the present case from the former erroneously settled one, they were on occasion quite broad-minded enough to say so.

At least three members of the Taney Court who concurred in one mistake agreed to the about-face, and one of them actually wrote the overruling opinion.

The point to be decided was the meaning of a clause in an 1830 act of Congress that established rules for the sale of public lands, which meant most of the land there was, and determined who would get it. Throughout much of the national territory, settlers had taken over and been confirmed in tracts that had little relation to the later division into the standard sections, one mile square. Congress therefore provided that where entire sections could not be sold as units because parts already were privately owned, the fractional plots should be disposed of in half or quarter sections wherever practicable. However, the "fractional" lands were not always so neatly available in the standard four pieces of a section, quarter-mile squares that could be labeled as northeast, southeast, northwest, and southwest quarters of Section such-and-such.

One irregular bit containing just over 200 acres—a quarter section is 160—lay in the town of St. Stephens, Alabama. It contained all of a southwest quarter section and a few acres in each of the northwest and southeast quarters. Shortly after the Act of 1830, it was granted in roughly equal parts divided by a straight line running from north to south to James Etheridge and W. D. Stone. Etheridge got 92.67 acres west of the line and Stone 110.50 acres east of it. The line almost evenly bisected the southwest quarter. Each grantee paid the going price per acre to the government, and both soon sold out.

When William L. Brown acquired the Etheridge portion, he and his lawyers claimed the whole southwest quarter under the act of 1830. They pointed out that the whole quarter had been vacant when Etheridge and Stone came along. Since Etheridge's grant had been a few months earlier in time, he should have received the desirable square because Congress clearly intended that such tracts were preferable to smaller fractions. That this would have left Stone with an oddly shaped, narrow strip that ran around the northern and eastern boundaries of the Etheridge grant, and would be relatively valueless, was too bad.

The case came to the Supreme Court in the January term of 1845 with Brown's lessee seeking to oust Stone's successors, Joseph Clements and Jonathan Hunt, from nearly two-thirds of their land. The lessee succeeded, too, although the Chief Justice dissented along with Justices John Catron and Peter Daniel. The Etheridge grant now consisted of the entire southwest quarter, 160 acres, while Stone's share shrank from 110 to about 43. The majority opinion indicated that the act of 1830 should be interpreted as meaning that fractional sections should be granted in quarters or halves wherever possible, not just practicable.

This had not been the interpretation of either the United States Land Office or the Attorney General. In actual practice, fractional sections had been divided into reasonably contiguous and compact tracts, much in the pattern of the Etheridge-Stone original grants, rather than strain for complete half or quarter sections when the result would be left-over bits and pieces of little use to anyone. The Land Office did not change its practice after the Supreme Court's ruling in *Brown's Lessee v. Clements and Hunt*. It continued to use common sense in subdividing fractional sections, and in due course a man named Gazzam became possessed of the Clements and Hunt property. He was as little impressed by the 1845 decision as the Land Office, and sued to recover the land that opinion took away, which now belonged to Elam Phillips.

During the period covered by this reversal, the United States had the greatest combined growth of population and territory in all its history. The two decades, 1840–1860, saw the largest proportional increase in population of any covered by the census except the very first, 1790–1800. In 1840–1850, the increase was 35.9 percent; in 1850–1860, 35.6 percent. Never again did it rise as much as 27 percent in a single decade. In this same twenty-year period, the land area doubled and the country spanned the continent. Furthermore, of the 1,234,381 square miles acquired in

Oregon, Texas, the Mexican cession of California, and the Gadsden Purchase, nearly 80 percent was public land owned by the Federal Government.

Gazzam v. Phillips Lessee was argued in 1858 before a Supreme Court that still contained six of its 1845 members, all three dissenters and Justices Samuel Nelson, John McLean, and Wayne. Nelson now wrote for a unanimous Court that the only difficulty he and his colleagues faced in allowing the Land Office rather than themselves to judge the practicality of subdivisions was the 1845 opinion in which he had concurred. He now pointed out that Stone had paid for 110 acres, not 43. He also mentioned that a strict adherence to the Court's 1845 decision would unsettle vast tracts of land granted all over the country during the last twenty-eight years in accordance with the doctrine that the Court had struck down and that apparently had been applied except to this one particular tract of 200-odd acres out of all the millions of acres being disposed of.

"We cannot, therefore, adopt that decision or apply its principles in rendering the judgment of the Court in this case," Nelson wrote in what is perhaps as explicit a profession of personal error as a Supreme Court justice has ever uttered.

So Gazzam got back the full 110 acres for which Stone had paid, and a great many other titles were more secure than they had been. Of course, the fact that adherence to the *Brown* rule would have caused great confusion in redrawing boundary lines was a factor in the 1858 decision. But if the justices had not been convinced of their earlier error, they probably would have forced Congress to make amends by a new statute confirming what the Land Office had done, and that too would have opened the doors to new litigation.

The overrulings so far described represent a departure from a precedent established in an earlier Supreme Court decision. But one type of about-face has itself become a precedent, with no confession or error or altered circumstances involved. An early classic example of this working of *stare decisis* in reverse settled the disposition of Mary Clarke's farm on the island of Manhattan, achieved fifty-eight years after she died in 1802.

Her farm took in a large part of a neighborhood called Chelsea, as it still is, which was then part of Greenwich Village, a community not yet incorporated into New York City. Mrs. Clarke's will provided that the land be held in trust, the income to be paid to her grandson, Thomas B. Clarke, "natural son of my late son Clement," for his lifetime. After his death, the property was to go outright to his children, if any. If he had no children, the farm would revert to another grandson, Clement Clarke Moore, who long before this case was finally settled wrote "'Twas the Night Before Christmas."

Thomas Clarke married in 1803 and during the next dozen years had six children, but lost his wife. The income from his grandmother's farm was sadly insufficient to maintain him in the way of life to which he had grown accustomed, and in 1814 and 1815 he persuaded the state legislature to permit him to sell some or all of the Chelsea land with the consent of the Court of Chancery. In his petition he pleaded that one reason he needed the money was that he had "an expensive family." In actual fact, although the legislature did not bother to inquire, he had no part in the care of his three surviving children. They were being raised by friends and relatives with no support from him. The private bills were enacted into law, whereupon Clarke sold the land in parcels, most of them apparently transferred to his various creditors to liquidate his debts, but in at least one instance for $3,750 in cash besides. The chancellor who approved these actions was James Kent, a jurist often ranked with such as Marshall and called "the American Blackstone." Clement Clarke Moore, who owned a good deal of New York real estate already, obligingly waived his rather remote claim to the property.

Clarke died in 1826, and his affairs became one of those long-drawn-out contests over wills and estates that have inspired loud condemnation of the law's delays from many laymen and some lawyers. The three Clarke children tried to recover the property their great-grandmother had intended for them, and after meeting several reversals in the state tribunals turned to the United States Circuit Court for the Southern District of New York. One of the children, Catharine, now the middle-aged wife of Charles A. Williamson, demanded that Joseph Berry be ejected from a part of the farm that he had bought from one of the Clarke creditors, proprietor of an oyster house where apparently Thomas Clarke had run up an astronomical bill. The Williamsons brought similar suits against the Irish Presbyterian Congregation and one Joseph Ball, successors to two other creditors.

The circuit court declined to look into the merits of a case that the state courts already had decided, but it referred the question of jurisdiction, and several other points of law, to the Supreme Court. There in 1850 Justice Wayne for himself and four colleagues said that it was quite proper for the United States to look into the matter of a state court's jurisdiction. He pointed out that the private bills authorizing the sale of the farm had said nothing about paying the father's debts but had said a great deal about using the proceeds for the benefit of the children. Wayne held that the chancellor exceeded his authority in permitting Clarke to sign away titles in repayment of his personal obligations, so the Williamsons were entitled not only to Berry's property but to that of the Congregation and Ball as well. Taney, Nelson, and Catron dissented.

Litigation of this kind often takes on a seeming immortality. One Supreme Court decision was by no means enough to kill the controversy over Mary Clarke's Chelsea farm, which on the eve of the Civil War was now well within New York City and worth enough to warrant indefinite legal wrangling. The population had gone from 515,000 to 800,000 in the single decade, 1850–1860, a rate of increase never equaled before or since. Millions of dollars were now at stake in what had been a farm incapable of supporting a gentleman. So the proprietors who held title from Clarke's creditors declined to accept eviction, and they continued to win their cases in the state courts. In its December term of 1860, the Supreme Court confronted a new aspect of the litigation in *Suydam v. Williamson.*

Suydam was the successor to Peter McIntyre, who had paid Clarke the $3,750 for his tract over and above the debt Clarke owed. When Williamson (Catharine's son) won a verdict against him in the United States Court for the Southern District of New York on the strength of *Berry,* Suydam appealed. A new member of the Court, Justice John Campbell, wrote for all of the seven members present at the time, including Wayne and Grier of the 1850 majority, that *Berry* was herewith overruled.

Justice Campbell admitted that Clarke never had used any of the money from the sale of the farm to support his children. But the New York courts knew this, too, and nevertheless had found for the purchasers as against the heirs. In fact, after *Berry,* the state's highest court had upheld the sales in outspoken contradiction of the gentlemen in Washington. The New York Court of Appeals had held that when any conflict exists between rulings of a New York court and a United States court, except in cases involving the national Constitution or laws, the state's court's decisions "are of controlling authority."

This state version, after all, was very like the position that Marshall's Court had taken when it reversed his interpretation of Tennessee's land law in 1832. A precedent of deference to the local interpretation of local laws virtually commanded an about-face in the matter of that old Chelsea farm. Campbell accepted it, and even tried to excuse the former decision, as McLean in 1832 had excused Marshall's of 1816, by saying the state's rule was not clear when the case first came up on appeal. Actually, the only divided opinion Campbell could find in this case was that within the United States circuit court. But his bow to precedent no doubt enabled Wayne and Robert Grier to execute their about-face with better grace.

∽ 5 ∽

Reversal by Appointment

Considering the convulsions through which the United States passed during and just after the Civil War, it is small surprise that perhaps the most convulsive about-face the Supreme Court ever made stemmed from that irrepressible conflict. This one did involve the construction of the Constitution, and the Court that had to do the construing was still recovering from an enormous blow to its prestige dealt in 1857 when, for the second time in history, it declared an act of Congress null and void. This ruling came in the course of deciding whether a slave named Dred Scott became free because his owner had taken him for five years into a free territory and then brought him back to St. Louis. Taney gave what came to be called the opinion of the Court, although all nine members wrote different versions. The net result was to strike down the Missouri Compromise by which Congress had confined slavery for more than thirty-five years south of latitude 30° 30′. The Chief Justice said Congress had no power to forbid the South's "peculiar institution" in any national territory; that could be done only when the territory became a state and by the new state itself.

This decision was denounced even more hotly than the first in which the Court had nullified an act of Congress. In that one, written in 1803, Marshall had avoided really serious conflict over his ruling by denying Congress a right his enemies did not claim for it. He held that Congress could not expand the powers of his Court beyond the limits set in the Constitution. On that ground, he refused to issue a writ against Secretary of State James Madison, who was defendant in the case but had ignored it and did not even send a representative to the hearing. Since he and President Jefferson complained that the Chief Justice was claiming more authority than the Constitution granted, they could hardly do more than blast his impertinence in arrogating to himself the right to say what the Court could not do.

Taney's opinion in 1857 was much more divisive. It opened all the territories to slavery and ended all hope of settling the issue peaceably. While it was not the sole or even the main cause of the war, it helped. It was so bitterly reviled and brought such contempt upon the Court that one of Taney's successors, Charles Evans Hughes, called the decision a "public calamity." Justice Felix Frankfurter said eighty years after the event that for years members of the Supreme Court were as shy of speaking of this decision as was the family of a hanged man about mentioning ropes. Dred Scott himself was set free by his abolitionist owner, who had financed the lawsuit, and died before the war broke out. Taney survived until late in 1864, long enough to see the slavery in which he believed doomed and the Court over which he had presided for twenty-seven years reach its lowest ebb in popular esteem.

The immense effort that the war required set the stage for the next Supreme Court nullification of an act of Congress, and for an unusually bitter about-face. The monetary and financial system of the United States was quite inadequate to support the armies and buy the supplies that a major war demanded. Under the tutelage of the Treasury Department, headed by Salmon P. Chase, who had been and remained one of Lincoln's chief Republican rivals, Congress raised a large part of the money needed by authorizing the Treasury to print paper money—the amount went to $450 million before the war was over—without any provision or promise to redeem it in gold or silver at any time. To keep these notes from going the way of Confederate money or the so-called Continentals of Revolutionary War fame, Congress stipulated that they should be legal tender. This meant that the Government would take them for taxes and that they must be accepted "in payment of all debts, public and private."

Because of the color of the ink in which the new currency was printed, the bills came quickly to be called "greenbacks."

The first act, authorizing $150 million, went into effect on February 25, 1862, and a wave of horror swept over the Eastern business and financial community. Until the war was over, nothing could be done, but then the theory that the Government's power to coin money included the power to print it, and make people take it, became a lively issue. Plenty of men of substance believed that the only conceivable lawful money was gold and silver or notes redeemable in gold or silver. Currency in the form of unsecured bank notes or Government bills might be a convenience but was intrinsically no more valuable than individuals' I.O.U.'s or promissory notes. If they circulated, let them find their own level in terms of hard money. Under these circumstances, the legality of "legal tender" was bound to reach the Supreme Court.

It arrived during the December term of 1863 by way of the New York Court of Appeals. A member of the Roosevelt family who held a mortgage on property owned by one Meyer had refused to take $8,171 in greenbacks as full payment. (Checking accounts as a routine method for paying bills were still in the future.) Roosevelt said the paper was worth only $7,844.22 at the time—it was much less by the end of 1863—and the lower state courts agreed he was entitled to the balance. But New York's highest tribunal upheld the Legal Tender Act, and Roosevelt appealed.

The justices sidestepped neatly. They found that they had no jurisdiction under the special circumstances of *Roosevelt v. Meyer*. The Judiciary Act seemed to them to say that when the highest courts of a state affirmed the constitutionality of a Federal law, the Supreme Court should not look further into the matter. If the state sought to nullify the law, then only did the Supreme Court have jurisdiction.

Taney and his colleagues no doubt shrank from passing on a vital war measure that most of them would have felt obliged to condemn, thus throwing the financial backing of the Union into chaos. By the time they could no longer avoid the decision, Taney had died and been succeeded in December 1864 by Chase, the Secretary of the Treasury whose department had issued the greenbacks. Before they faced the crucial issues, he and his associates pronounced a unanimous overruling that indicated a new judicial attitude toward ways of doing business in the United States. In the process, they reflected changed concepts of commercial obligations between the day of Jefferson and Marshall and that of President Grant and Chief Justice Chase.

In 1867, when *Mason v. Eldred* et al. appeared on the Court's December docket, commerce and industry had become more important than shipping and agriculture in the American economy. A nation of 31 millions spanning a continent had little use for many of the trading mores that in 1810 served a country of 7 millions, for most of whom Illinois was the Far West and which had the fewest people per square mile, 4.3, since before the first census of 1790.

In those simpler days, Marshall had ruled that all members of a business partnership were liable for the debts of the firm. The specific obligation he talked about had been incurred on July 17, 1804, when James Sheehy took a note signed by Robert Brown Jamesson, a merchant of Alexandria, Virginia, in payment for $604.91 worth of goods. Sheehy failed to collect, and when he finally won a court judgment against Jamesson in 1806, the merchant was protected by a law "for the relief of insolvent debtors." Then Sheehy learned that Joseph Mandeville, who was not insolvent, had been Jamesson's silent partner. The creditor sued in the United States court in Alexandria, but lost when the judge upheld Mandeville's plea that a judgment against one partner clears the other. If Mandeville had been named in the same action as Jamesson, he would have been liable, but (the argument ran in effect) a creditor can take only one shot at a debtor partnership.

Sheehy appealed, and Marshall in 1810 found him amply justified, saying: "In point of real justice, there can be no reason why an unsatisfied judgment against Jamesson should bar a claim upon Mandeville; and it appears to the Court that this claim is not barred by any technical rule of law."

However reasonable that opinion may seem, the idea of a creditor tracking down one partner after another to collect a debt was unpalatable in many parts of the country, and among many debtors. While the Federal courts appear to have followed Marshall faithfully, state judges sometimes flouted his opinion, and shortly after the Civil War the United States Circuit Court in Wisconsin confessed itself unable to rule on *Mason v. Eldred* et al.

Mason had sued Elisha Eldred in Michigan on a partnership note signed by him, his brother Anson, and one Balcom. Only Elisha had been served. He alone appeared in court. Mason won a verdict, but could not collect. Thereupon, he sued Anson Eldred in the

Federal court in Wisconsin, citing *Sheehy v. Mandeville*, and from there the case came to the Supreme Court. Justice Stephen J. Field, in the name of eight members of the Court present, decided:

> A judgment against one upon a joint contract of several persons, bars an action against the others, though the latter were dormant partners of the defendant in the original action, and this fact was unknown to the plaintiff when that action was commenced.

Justice Field took special note of *Mandeville* to explain why the Court was not following it.

"The decision in this case," he asserted, "has never received the entire approbation of the profession, and its correctness has been doubted and its authority disregarded in numerous instances by the highest tribunals of different states."

He then proceeded to recite examples from New York, Massachusetts, Illinois, Maryland, Indiana, and Pennsylvania. He observed that most of these state courts made the by now conventionally polite bow to the respect due the pronouncements of the Supreme Court. Field also quoted the English Court of Exchequer where a barrister had pleaded the *Mandeville* precedent unsuccessfully. The English judges had expressed "the greatest respect for any decision of Chief Justice Marshall," but had called the reasoning attributed to him in this case unsatisfactory. Field agreed with both encomiums and the overruling.

Clearly, the principle that a partner remains responsible for partnership debts even if he has escaped detection at first was not compatible with postwar ways of doing business. This, after all, was the era of Jim Fiske, Jay Gould, Daniel Drew, and hundreds like them in the corporate world, and of such congressional leaders as James Blaine and James A. Garfield, whose political careers were not even interrupted by the revelation that they could be bought for a few shares of stock. Successful concealment of assets from a creditor was hardly likely to offend the consciences of men who could accept the public and private ethics of the most brazen generation of boodlers in American history and elevate some of the worst of the lot to positions of honor and trust.

This was the prevailing moral climate when the Supreme Court came to consider legal tender. The justices heard counsels' arguments in the same term in which they decided *Mason v. Eldred*, but they took a great deal longer to reach a decision, for the Court has seldom been more bitterly divided. Three members were left from the Taney court, Justices Grier, Nelson, and Clifford. The wartime appointments, besides Chase himself, a somewhat embittered politician, were Samuel Freeman Miller of Iowa, appointed in 1862—the first justice from west of the Mississippi; David Davis of Illinois, also appointed in 1862, Lincoln's friend, roommate on the Illinois circuit, and 1860 campaign manager; Stephen Johnson Field, member of a distinguished Eastern legal family who had moved to California and become the new state's chief justice before Lincoln appointed him to the Supreme Court in 1863, one of the few members to serve the Marshall span of thirty-four years; and Noah H. Swayne of Ohio, the first Lincoln appointment. Swayne and Miller took the seats of justices who had resigned to join the Confederacy.

The bone of contention thrown to this group in 1867 had been well gnawed in the lower courts. It reached Washington from Kentucky, where Henry Griswold of Louisville had been trying to collect a debt under circumstances that raised just the right points for a test. It contained all the elements the enemies of greenbacks thought they needed to prove their case.

Back in the halcyon days of peace, on June 20, 1860, a Mrs. Hepburn had given Griswold a note promising to pay him on February 20, 1862, "the sum of eleven thousand two hundred and fifty dollars." When the day came, five days before the first greenback Legal Tender Bill became law, she did not pay, but for a time the creditor was not pressing. After the war, however, he filed a suit in the Kentucky Court of Chancery. Before it came to trial, Mrs. Hepburn offered Griswold $12,750 in greenbacks, the sum representing the $11,250 principal, and accrued interest of $1,500 since 1862. Griswold said the word "dollars" in Mrs. Hepburn's promissory note meant the standard gold or silver of that time, and he insisted on going ahead with his lawsuit.

The Court of Chancery held that the Legal Tender Act fitted this case perfectly, and that Mrs. Hepburn had discharged her debt with greenbacks. Griswold appealed to the Kentucky Court of Errors, which said no, a creditor need not accept greenbacks if he did not like them, especially if the debt was supposed to have been paid before the law's effective date. This time it was Mrs. Hepburn's turn to appeal.

Congressional ambivalence toward the Court during the 1860s accounted for the membership of eight at this time. In March 1863, the size was fixed at ten, and Field was appointed. Then on July 23, 1866, Congress decreed that no vacancies be filled until the Court had shrunk to a chief justice and six associate justices. Only two vacancies had occurred since then. (Before the final reduction was complete, Congress changed its mind again and authorized nine—the rule for more than a century—the measure to become effective on the first Monday in December 1869.)

The eight who listened to the first legal tender argument, fresh from their unanimous *Eldred* decision, were well aware that they held sharply divergent views on this new issue. Some of them indicated a feeling of relief when the Attorney General asked for an opportunity to be heard as a Friend of the Court, in view of the great importance of the case, to which the Government was not of course a party. They set *Hepburn v. Griswold* for reargument in the December 1868 term. By then other legal tender appeals were on the docket, so that a total of fifteen lawyers, including some of the most eminent and a few of the most learned in the country, addressed the Court. All in all, the issue was discussed with uncommon fervor and skill.

This period was not only "the golden age of graft," but the era of Reconstruction, one of the most turbulent in the political annals of the country. Between the time the Supreme Court heard the first and second set of arguments on the first legal tender case, the following events had taken place: The House of Representatives had impeached President Johnson for firing his Secretary of War without the consent of the Senate and that body, by one vote, failed to convict him. (Years later the Supreme Court ruled unconstitutional the law he was accused of violating.) Grant had been elected President over Horatio Seymour by a popular vote of 3,000,000 to 2,700,000 and an electoral vote of 214 to 80. Adoption of the Fourteenth Amendment was proclaimed after North and South Carolina reversed an earlier rejection.

By the time the Court finally decided the legal tender issue, the Fifteenth Amendment had been ratified and Congress got its first Negro members in both houses; Wall Street had its "Black Friday" gold panic; the first railroad to the Pacific was completed; and the territory of Wyoming took the pioneer step of enfranchising women.

Far and away the most distinguished pleader was President Johnson's new Attorney General, William M. Evarts. He had prosecuted Jefferson Davis for treason and lost, and defended the President at his impeachment trial and won. A future Secretary of State and United States Senator, he had an enormous reputation for both eloquence and legal skill. He and the other fourteen exhausted their subject if not the patience of the Court, for they repeated themselves and each other endlessly. If any of them changed the opinion of a single judge, no hint of it appears in the record. When it came to the point, each of the eight men on the bench had to decide what he thought certain words in the Constitution meant, and they were such common words that not even an Evarts was likely to come up with a new definition that would alter a competent judge's understanding of these passages from Article I, Section 10 on the powers of Congress:

To borrow Money on the credit of the United States . . .

To regulate Commerce with foreign Nations, and among the several States, and with the Indian Tribes . . .

To coin Money, regulate the value thereof . . .

To raise and support Armies . . . To provide and maintain a Navy . . .

To make all Laws which shall be necessary and proper for carrying into Execution the foregoing Powers, and all other Powers vested by this Constitution in the Government of the United States, or in any Department or Officer thereof.

In addition, they had to interpret a clause in Section 10: "No State shall . . . make any Thing but gold and silver Coin a Tender in Payment of Debts," and the last clause of the Fifth Amendment, "nor shall private property be taken for public use, without just compensation."

No one at the bar or on the bench questioned the authority of Congress to print currency and call it money. The real issue was whether Congress could also make that money legal tender. Was that "necessary and proper" for carrying out the powers enumerated? The Federal Government possessed only those stated in the Constitution? John Marshall was supposed to have given the definitive answer to this question in 1819 when he went a little out of his way in ruling that Congress had authority to set up a bank. In telling the legal profession what "necessary and proper" meant, he gave this classic definition of "implied powers":

Let the end be legitimate, let it be within the scope of the Constitution, and all means which are appropriate, which are plainly adapted to that end, which are not prohibited but consist [sic] with the letter and spirit of the Constitution, are constitutional.

Even earlier, in 1804, he had said that a law did not have to be "indispensably necessary" to achieve the legitimate end. He was then upholding the right of Congress to make the United States a preferred creditor in settling the affairs of a bankrupt. He pointed out that few laws could be defended as the sole possible means for achieving their objectives, and therefore: "Congress must possess the choice of means."

Not one of the eight members of the Court in 1868 hinted at any desire to overrule these pronouncements. Each asserted that his reasoning flowed directly from the Marshall opinions. But they were far from unanimous in applying the great man's wisdom to the particular circumstances of Griswold's claim on Mrs. Hepburn.

They debated their various points of view for months, and at last, at a conference on November 27, 1869, they agreed to disagree. On January 29, 1870, they directed that their various opinions be read, and this was done on February 7. Meanwhile Grier, who had suffered a partial paralysis in the summer of 1867, had been growing progressively feebler. He wrote with great difficulty, and although the Chief Justice, with whom he agreed at this time, said his mind was clear, others saw in him plain indications of senility. He sat on the bench for the last time two days after the opinion was ordered read and resigned on February 1, leaving lawyers to argue heatedly and futilely whether or not a full Court had reached the decision announced.

When Chase read the opinion of the Court that February day, he emphasized that he was authorized to speak for Grier as well as for Nelson, Clifford, and Field, so that a clear majority of five was behind the ruling. He speedily set Griswold's mind at ease by saying in his first few sentences that the Legal Tender Act could apply "only to debts contracted subsequent to the enactment of the law," since before that only gold and silver were legal tender. He then proceeded to say why making greenbacks legal tender did not meet Marshall's criterion of implied powers, which he took to mean "not absolutely necessary, indeed, but appropriate." The means were inappropriate in this case, he found, because, for one thing, they had not worked. He pointed out that by July 1864, these bills were so far from being accepted generally that it took $2.85 in greenbacks to buy a gold dollar, although "recently" the price had gone to $1.20. Other notes issued by the Government at the same time to help finance the war circulated at about the same discount. So the legal tender provision was not appropriate for its purpose, whether in carrying on the war, borrowing money, regulating the value of coined money, or regulating commerce. In effect, the Court decreed a "floating dollar," of which the country would hear more in a hundred years.

Furthermore, the Chief Justice declared, Congress had violated the Fifth Amendment. Compelling a citizen to take less for money or any other consideration advanced before the passage of the act was a sort of confiscation. At the low point of greenbacks in 1864, this amounted to "taking" nearly two-thirds of the value of a creditor's property. Prosecution of the war was a public purpose, and a laudable one, but the Government was still obliged to pay "just compensation" if it wanted people to take its currency at face value.

Chase did not mention his own share in making greenbacks legal tender. He contented himself with affirming the ruling of the Kentucky Court of Errors in favor of Griswold. When he finished, Justice Miller read a dissent in which Swayne and Davis concurred. The burden of their argument was that the legal tender provision was well within the limits of congressional choice in these matters, especially in choice of means to carry on a war and to regulate the value of the currency. He also pointed out that the Constitution forbade only the states to make anything except gold and silver legal tender. Because the prohibition did not extend to the Federal Government, he contended, the Constitution clearly implied ample power to justify the law of 1862.

The majority decision dealt a severe shock to the country's money system, still shaky from the effects of a "Black Friday" the previous fall when Jay Gould and Jim Fiske nearly cornered the gold market. Greenbacks constituted a large part of the currency of the country, and an ample supply of reasonably stable money seemed essential to the great postwar expansion to which everyone looked forward now that the first railroad to the west coast had been completed. The great event took place while the justices were trying to compose their legal tender opinion. As a result of that opinion merchants and manufacturers, importers and exporters, bankers and shippers were expressing fears for the future of the economy.

These reactions might have been more serious if President Grant had not been able to remodel the Supreme Court within a matter of weeks. With Grier's resignation and the effective date of the nine-man bench at hand, he could name two new members. Even as the news of the decision went out over the telegraph, a prompt reversal seemed possible. Within a few hours, it was probable.

The opportunity for such timely appointments comes seldom to a President. When it does, can he be sure his man will construe the Constitution and the laws as his appointer would do? Lincoln had expressed this dilemma when he was considering the nomination of Chase. He wanted, he said, "a Chief Justice who will sustain what has been done in regard to emancipation and the legal tenders." Yet only five years later, here was Chase declaring legal tender invalid.

"We cannot ask a man what he will do," Lincoln had said in that same statement, "and if we should, and he should answer us, we should despise him for it. Therefore, we must take a man whose opinions are known."

Grant succeeded better than Lincoln. The day Chase delivered the Court's decision, the President sent to the Senate the names of William Strong, who as a Pennsylvania Supreme Court judge had written an opinion upholding the validity of the legal tender laws, and Joseph P. Bradley, a New Jersey railroad lawyer, who would hardly be less friendly than Strong. By March 21, 1870, the two new justices were sworn in—appointed and confirmed with exceptional promptness.

Over the somewhat bitter protests of the Chief Justice and his three remaining supporters, the new majority promptly agreed to hear two new appeals for the avowed purpose of reconsidering the whole issue. Never before nor since has an overruling been so promptly and frankly initiated by the appointment of men whose views were known to oppose an opinion of the Court. When argument was set for the following December, the result could hardly be doubted.

The lawsuits selected were very like *Hepburn* in essentials, but sufficiently different in detail to appease upholders of precedent who can take comfort from the old maxim, "circumstances alter cases." The first, and the one that led to an exceptionally long record of judicial opinions—230 closely printed pages—was *Knox v. Lee*. It was, as *Hepburn* had been, a dispute between a man and a woman.

Mrs. Lee, described as "a loyal citizen of the United States resident in Pennsylvania," had owned 608 sheep in Texas when the war broke out. The Confederate Government confiscated the animals as enemy property and sold them to Knox. When the war ended, Mrs. Lee sued him for $15,000, which she said was the value of the flock. Under the system by which judges and juries were chosen in the Reconstruction South, an ex-rebel's defense that he had bought the sheep in good faith from a *de facto* government was not expected to be considered seriously. Even he and his lawyers were resigned to the fact that he would have to pay Mrs. Lee. The question that chiefly concerned them was how much.

Counsel for Mrs. Lee wanted gold or its equivalent, and offered to prove the difference in value between paper and hard money. The judge declined, but in his charge to the jury, he told them that any award they made to Mrs. Lee would be payable in greenbacks. Knox protested that this was an invitation to set a high figure.

Without this invidious judicial remark, he said, the jury would not have given Mrs. Lee a verdict nearly as large as the $7,368 they set as the value of the sheep. His appeal was to get a ruling on the judge's charge, but in the process the Supreme Court could take up the constitutionality of the Legal Tender Act.

The other case, *Parker v. Davis*, concerned a prewar contract for the transfer of a tract of land in Massachusetts. Parker had agreed to sell, but when Davis offered him greenbacks after the first Legal Tender Act, he refused to give up title. One Massachusetts court declined to let him cancel the contract unilaterally. Another told him he had to sell at the agreed price and accept greenbacks. Parker appealed from this court's order that he transfer title to Davis.

The 1870 arguments covered the same ground as those of 1868. After counsel for the interested parties had been heard, the judges agreed to listen to further discussion of the constitutional issue from one eminent lawyer on the winning side in *Hepburn*, Clarkson N. Potter, and from Grant's current Attorney General, Amos T. Akerman. These two spoke at length without adding anything that had not been said before, consuming the Court's sitting of April 18, 1871, and the justices retired to conference. They emerged on May 1 with the expected decision that the Legal Tender Acts were constitutional on the grounds that Miller had stated the previous year. This time Chase wrote the chief dissenting opinion for himself, Nelson, Clifford, and Field, with the last two reading further dissents. Bradley added a concurring opinion of his own to Strong's opinion of the Court. The actual delivery of all of them was put off until January 15, 1872, "to promote the convenience of some of the dissentient members of the Court."

Presidents have sometimes wished they could follow the Grant example and rush enough judges to the Supreme Court to overturn rulings the Chief Executive dislikes. None has yet been able to do it so blatantly, and in one respect perhaps they were fortunate. Grant and his advisers and the new Court majority all incurred a good deal of caustic criticism for casting doubt on the impartiality of the Supreme Court. Better to allow an erroneous doctrine to stand, these critics said, than put the Court in the position of seeming to bend to political considerations. Strong anticipated this when he explained in his *Knox v. Lee* opinion why the majority was in such a hurry to make the Court's about-face.

"Even in cases involving only private rights, if convinced we had made a mistake, we would hear another argument and correct our error," he said. "We agree this should not be done inconsiderately, but in a case of such far-reaching consequences as the present, thoroughly convinced as we are that Congress has not transgressed its powers, we regard it as our duty so to decide."

The following December, the Court decided that it also had made a mistake in its 1863 interpretation of the Judiciary Act. In spite of *Roosevelt v. Meyer*, Justice Field wrote for the Court, it did have jurisdiction over *Trebilcock v. Wilson* et ux., an appeal from a legal tender decision of the Iowa Supreme Court.

Wilson, in June 1861, had given Trebilcock a promissory note for $900 "payable in specie" with interest at 10 percent. As security, Wilson and his wife signed a mortgage on some land they owned. The creditor refused to accept payment in greenbacks in February 1863, nor would he release the mortgage. In July 1865, Wilson won a court order canceling the mortgage while the greenbacks were left for Trebilcock to pick up whenever he wished. The state supreme court affirmed this ruling, and when Trebilcock took an appeal to Washington, the Wilsons pleaded *Roosevelt v. Meyer* to get the case thrown out.

Justice Field revealed that the 1863 ruling was based on only one clause of the Judiciary Act. Another clause, he now discovered, conferred jurisdiction over state court interpretations of Federal laws whether or not these had been favorable to the Government. He and six other members had served on the Court at the time, but none tried to explain how or why they had overlooked the passage in the Judiciary Act on which they now relied.

Having achieved this about-face, seven justices, with Bradley and Miller dissenting, decided that when a contract specifically called for payment in specie, the debtor would have to deliver coin or its equivalent. The great legal tender controversy petered out with the greenbacks just where they always had been, fluctuating in value as against gold or silver in accordance with confidence in the economy. But a decisive constitutional issue had been settled. Congress does possess power over the monetary system.

∽ 6 ∽

Outlawing the Income Tax

The Supreme Court continued to about-face through the 1870s and '80s on technical points where Federal laws were concerned, and in deference to state courts when local laws were at issue. Land continued to be the basis for most of the litigation, although corporations were accounting for ever larger fractions. By far the majority of the nation's wealth was still real estate. The census of 1890 undertook to list the "true value" of all real and personal property in the country, and if it was accurate you could have bought it all for much less than half of the Federal Government's current budget for a year. The census figure was just over $65 billion, of which $39.5 billion represented land and improvements.

Lawyers and judges, therefore, kept busy with mortgages, titles, surveys, wills, damages by trespass or otherwise to farms, and a host of other earthy disputes.

Typical of problems that these decades brought was a wrangle from Montana that reached the Supreme Court in 1873. A farmer named Toombs sued another, Hornbuckle, for depriving him of irrigation by diverting a stream. In the territorial courts—statehood was still sixteen years away—Toombs won one dollar in damages, but also an injunction entitling him to seventy inches of water from the stream. Hornbuckle appealed on the ground that the territorial court was illegally organized. He had four Supreme Court decisions to back him up, all handed down in the last eleven years, and one of them originating in Montana, although the territorial government was only nine years old. The decisions were based on an act of Congress of 1792 setting up rules for the territories. The rule that led to *Toombs v. Hornbuckle* and the other cases had not been changed by later laws amending other parts. It provided that all territories must have courts with both common law jurisdiction and equity jurisdiction. (Equity in the United States is a system of rules that is used to supplement statute and common law when these last do not fairly cover a case, or to provide relief for unforeseen hardships.)

In *Noonan v. Lee* in 1862 and three later decisions, the Supreme Court had held that this meant separate courts for equity and law. The first dispute was an attempt by Lee to make Noonan pay for city lots he had contracted to buy in a place called Mechanicsville in Wisconsin in 1855, and for which he had given a mortgage. Lee wanted to foreclose the mortgage and also get a court order requiring Noonan to pay him the difference between the proceeds of a new sale of the land and the 1855 contract price—a considerable difference since it now seemed doubtful that Mechanicsville existed. Contradictory surveys and missing city plats complicated the issue, but in the end the United States court in Wisconsin gave Lee what he wanted. The Supreme Court reversed that part of the verdict which said Noonan had to pay more than the land brought. The district judge had no power to make such an award because he was not entitled to rule on both law and equity. When Hornbuckle's counsel cited this decision, he found the 1873 Court facing the other way.

"On a careful review of the whole subject," said Justice Bradley for the Court, "we are not satisfied that those decisions are founded on a correct view of the law."

Apparently, the Court had done a little historical research on the act of 1792. At that time several states combined law and equity in a single court, and some did not. Members of Congress who drew up the statute, mostly lawyers then as now, were well aware of that. When they decreed that territorial courts should have both common law and equity jurisdiction, they did not mean to require that these be lodged in separate tribunals. Discretion on this point was left to the territorial legislature that established the courts. *Noonan v. Lee* and the other three cases, all decided unanimously, were overruled by a bare majority. Clifford, Davis, and Strong dissented, and one vote was missing. This was the vote of the Chief Justice, for Chase died earlier that year and was not replaced until the next because the Senate rejected President Grant's first three nominations as grossly unfit.

Another about-face of the period, and one that was not concerned with land or property of any kind, set some standards for the rights of witnesses before committees of Congress.

When the great banking house of Jay Cooke & Co., which had done a large part of the Civil War financing, collapsed under the weight of postwar corruption and speculation, the United States Government was one of the big losers. During the revelations that followed, a rumor circulated that a real estate pool had secretly salvaged substantial assets for a group of insiders. Responding to popular indignation, the House of Representatives passed a resolution on January 24, 1876, authorizing the Speaker, Michael C. Kerr, to appoint a committee to investigate settlement of

United States claims against the defunct Cooke bank, although a Federal court in Philadelphia was already wrestling with the bankrupt's affairs.

The committee subpoenaed Hallett Kilbourne, a Cooke associate, who was supposed to have information about the real estate deals. He appeared without the papers the subpoena called for, and he refused to answer when asked to supply the names and addresses of five members of the real estate pool. The full House voted to have the sergeant-at-arms bring him before that body on March 4, 1876, and, when he remained obdurate, ordered him held in the District of Columbia jail for contempt. He spent forty-five days there on a warrant signed by the Speaker, and when he got out he instituted a suit for false arrest and imprisonment, *Kilbourne v. Thompson* et al., that took more than four years to settle.

The first defendant was John G. Thompson, the sergeant-at-arms. The others were the Speaker and four members of the committee. Kilbourne lost in the district court, but found more sympathy in the Supreme Court, when he finally got his case there in October 1880. His position was that the Constitution gave Congress no power to punish anyone for contempt. The House not only claimed such power, but argued that the courts must presume Congress exercised it properly.

Justice Miller, speaking for the Court, took a middle course. He said that some power for Congress to protect itself is implied in the Constitution. But this gave Congress no explicit authority to punish anyone for anything except its own members and, by impeachment, Government officials. "We are sure no person can be punished for contumacy as a witness before either House," he added, "unless his testimony is required in a matter into which that House has jurisdiction to inquire, and we feel equally sure that neither of these bodies possesses the general power of making inquiry into the private affairs of the citizen. . . . At this point in our inquiry, we are met by *Anderson v. Dunn.*"

The note of regret detectable in this last statement deepened as

Justice Miller went on to overrule this decision that had, nearly sixty years earlier, in 1821, dismissed the complaint of another man haled before the bar of the House. On January 8, 1818, Sergeant-at-arms Thomas Dunn brought John Anderson into the House, "gently," Dunn claimed—on a warrant signed by Speaker Henry Clay. Without further ceremony, the members voted him guilty of "a breach of the privileges of the said House, and of a high contempt of its dignity and authority." Nowhere in the surviving documents is the nature of Anderson's offense stated, but language in the reported summary of the case suggests that he had tried to bribe a congressman. For two months he remained in Dunn's custody. Finally, he was brought back to the bar of the House "and there reprimanded by the said Speaker for the outrage by the said John committed." After this verbal punishment, he was discharged from custody and promptly sued Dunn for trespass. As happened to Kilbourne nearly sixty years later, the district court ruled against him, and he appealed.

Justice William Johnson, who wrote the opinion of the Supreme Court, noted, as did Miller, that Congressional power to punish for contempt was only implied in the Constitution. He considered it broad enough to cover this case, for he was willing to accept the judgment of the House of Representatives.

"There is nothing on the face of this record from which it can appear on what evidence the warrant was issued," he said. "And we are not to presume that the House of Representatives would have issued it without duly establishing the fact charged on the individual."

However justified this faith may have been in 1821, the Supreme Court was not prepared to presume it in 1880. Miller softened the blow by suggesting that the 1821 decision was influenced by the practice of the British House of Commons, which for centuries had been summarily committing to prison people who offended it. In fact, Justice Johnson had cited some of these precedents. Now, reported Miller, naming cases, the Commons had modified this practice a good deal, and in any case that House was not nearly so limited in its authority as an American Congress. Since the papers our Representatives wanted from Kilbourne and the questions they asked concerned his private affairs that affected no legitimate business of Congress, he had been wronged.

That did not mean, Miller hastened to add, that Kilbourne could obtain redress from Speaker Kerr and the four members of the committee named as defendants. The Constitution protected these individuals even more effectively than it protected Kilbourne. For it said members of Congress "shall not be questioned in any other place" for anything they did in their official capacities. This blanket immunity did not cover the sergeant-at-arms, so the decision remanded the case against Thompson to the District of Columbia court to be considered on its merits, but only against him.

A more typical about-face was an 1889 opinion over the seizure of a shipment of beer in Iowa. It specifically overruled an 1847 decision concerning a barrel of gin. (We say "typical" rather than "representative" because alcoholic beverages did not occupy all that great a share of the Court's attention.)

In the 1847 case, Andrew and Thomas Pierce of Dover, New Hampshire, wholesalers, brought from out of state a barrel of Holland gin and sold it to Aaron Sias, price $11.85. New Hampshire law authorized town selectmen to require anyone who sold liquor to get a license from them. The Pierces held that this could not apply to a sale in its original package of a product brought from another state, because only Congress could regulate interstate commerce. The Taney court gave the Pierces short shrift, saying the regulation was well within the police power as long as it did not actually conflict with any act of Congress in the commerce field. This one did not.

On the strength of that decision, A. J. Hardin, town marshal of

Keokuk, Iowa, seemed to be justified when he confiscated a shipment of beer brought by Gus. Leisy & Co. from their brewery in
Peoria, Illinois. Iowa had recently outlawed such beverages, and
the state courts, all the way to the highest, brushed aside the plea
that interstate commerce was inviolable, at least until the beer got
into the lands of Leisy's customers. This time the Supreme Court
saw a great deal of merit in the dealer's contention. Whatever
rights the State of Iowa might have over beer within its borders,
these could come into play only after the original containers had
been sold. As long as Congress placed no obstacle in the way of
any commodity crossing state lines, Iowa would have to accept that
commodity.

"The authority of *Pierce v. New Hampshire* ... must be
regarded as having been distinctly overthrown," the opinion
concluded.

Such changes of the Court's mind attracted little attention outside of the legal profession—or even within it. But as the United
States entered the last decade of the nineteenth century, the
Supreme Court was once more headed toward a major about-face
on a constitutional issue that was of great popular interest. The
groundwork for this one was laid by the growing necessities of
government in dealing with new conditions. The wealth and
power of a generation of tycoons described as "the robber barons"
contrasted unpleasantly with enlarging aspirations of the people.
Demands of labor for the right to organize and profound rural
dissatisfaction with loss of domination to what Jefferson had called
the running sores of big cities put pressure for reforms on Congress.

These were the decades in which the states began regulation of
railroads and of a few other businesses "affected with a public
interest," a phrase the Supreme Court in a key decision upholding
regulation borrowed from a seventeenth-century Lord Chief Justice of England, Sir Matthew Hale. The first curbs on the right of

men to do as they pleased with their own property followed the panic of 1873 as well as revelations of corporate managers as corrupters on a scale that gave the name of "golden age of graft" to the whole era.

At the same time, population finally began to slow its breathless rate of increase. The decade of the 1890s was the first in which it fell below 2½ percent a year—from 1850-1890 it had averaged 4 percent. By contrast, for all our lowered death rate, the increase during the 1960s was less than 1½ percent a year.

The total population was estimated at about 70 millions when in 1895 the Supreme Court looked back at the earliest case it has ever overruled, *Hylton v. U.S.*, heard and decided at its seventh session, 1796, while the capital was still Philadelphia and the population less than 5 millions. The stake was the fledgling Government's ability to raise money, and taxation is always one matter that the legislative, executive, and judicial branches argue hotly. The particular tax under review was a levy Congress had attempted to put on horse-drawn carriages in 1794, a forerunner of the Federal automobile tax.

A government's need for money varies greatly, of course, with what it tries to do. In the early years of the Republic this was not much. The United States in 1796 had no national program of public works, no subsidies to education or farmers or utilities, and no parks. In this last full year of Washington's administration, it spent $5,727,000—only a little more than two-thirds of the $8,378,000 it raised. The post office paid for itself with letters carried for 6 cents within 30 miles, increasing to 25 cents over 450 miles. City delivery was extra, a fee paid to the letter carrier. The next year, an emergency defense budget to increase the army, navy, and coastal fortifications against the dangers of involvement in Europe's war was put at $1,500,000. Politics were old-fashioned. In the first contested Presidential election, fought in 1796, neither Adams nor Jefferson deigned to campaign actively. A mark of legislative enlightenment was an act providing that no

Federal court should order any man imprisoned for debt if he owed less than thirty dollars.

The plaintiff was a remarkably versatile litigant, Daniel Hylton, a man of many and varied interests. He had two completely different test cases, each involving a vital question of constitutional interpretation, that were not only heard at this term but were argued on successive days. Hylton, a Virginian, was a staunch upholder of the new Government, a big landowner and a leading merchant. He appeared in the latter capacity in the first of his two cases, *Ware v. Hylton*. His spokesman was John Marshall, then beginning to rival Patrick Henry at the Virginia bar. Some of Marshall's biographers think he laid the foundation of his national reputation in this lawsuit, which he lost, however.

The background of the case, on which depended the ownership of vast tracts of land and enormous sums owed by merchants, was this: William Jones, an Englishman, sued in United States court to collect on a bond for £2,976, 11s, 6d, executed to him and his late partner, Joseph Farrell, also a British subject, on July 7, 1774. Daniel Hylton & Co. refused to pay because the sovereign state of Virginia during the war had adopted a law releasing all loyal citizens from any debts owed to Britishers. But by the Treaty of Peace in 1783, the United States undertook to let British creditors collect honest debts, and the Constitution made treaties a higher law of the land than state statutes.

Hylton won in the lower court, as expected, and since Jones had died, the suit was pressed in the name of his executor, Ware. At the appeal in Philadelphia, lawyers argued for six days. The best Marshall could do was a plea that the Constitution could not allow Virginia law to be upset retroactively by a treaty. The simple answer was that the treaty did make the debt provision retroactive, and the Constitution is silent on the subject.

Hylton's stake in the next case on the docket was sixteen dollars. It was probably as synthetic a lawsuit as the Supreme Court has ever heard. Congress had enacted the carriage tax on June 5, 1794, and in the May term of the United States circuit court of Virginia, Hylton and the United States Attorney presented themselves with a "statement of facts" upon which they had agreed. One fact was that Hylton had not paid the tax. Another was that they waived a jury trial. The statement then proceeded:

"That the Defendant, as of the 5th day of June 1794 and therefrom to the last day of September following, owned, possessed, and kept 125 chariots for the conveyance of persons, and no more: That the chariots were kept exclusively for the Defendant's own private use, and not to let out to hire, or for the conveyance of persons for hire."

If the court found for the United States, the statement added, "Judgment shall be entered for the Plaintiff for two thousand dollars, to be discharged on the payment of sixteen dollars, the amount of the tax and penalty."

The tongue-in-cheek bit about 125 carriages was designed to get the sum at issue up to the Supreme Court's minimum. Hylton's reservation to settle for sixteen dollars if he lost was a prudent precaution to which the Government readily agreed in order to get a test case that would go all the way. The elaborate subterfuge was designed to determine whether this particular kind of tax was within the categories permitted by the Constitution. Any direct Federal tax had to be apportioned among the several states in proportion to population. If the carriage tax was a direct tax, the Government would have to bill each state for its share of the amount desired and rely on them to raise it by taxing carriages within their borders—a method found highly unsatisfactory during the Confederation.

At this time, the Federal judiciary operated under the original act of Congress creating it. It consisted of a Supreme Court of six members, a chief justice and five associates; thirteen district courts; and three circuit courts, each of which included two Supreme Court justices, although both were seldom present at the same sitting. The Virginia circuit judges divided evenly on the constitutionality of the carriage tax. In order to expedite a final ruling, Hylton "confessed judgment" and promptly entered an appeal from that judgment.

When the Supreme Court turned from *Ware v. Hylton* to *Hylton v. U.S.* the judges were treated to even more distinguished counsel than had appeared during the previous six days. The Government had employed Alexander Hamilton, recently resigned from Washington's Cabinet to enter the practice of law, to assist Attorney General Charles Lee, brother of Light Horse Harry and uncle of Robert E. Speaking for Hylton were Alexander Campbell, a leader of the Virginia bar who had also represented him in the previous case along with Marshall, and the Attorney General of Pennsylvania, Jared Ingersoll. Hamilton and Ingersoll had been members of the Constitutional Convention of 1787.

The bench they addressed was even more plentifully supplied with veterans of that select band. The new Chief Justice, Oliver Ellsworth of Connecticut; William Paterson of New Jersey; and James Wilson of Pennsylvania had been among the leaders who hammered out the compromises that made the Constitution viable. Ellsworth, however, was sworn in only the morning the hearing began and took no part in the decision. The two other judges who did were Samuel Chase of Maryland, a ferocious Federalist partisan chiefly remembered as the only Supreme Court justice to be impeached (he was acquitted) but at this time with only a few days' service on the Court, and James Iredell of North Carolina, a member almost from the start. The fifth associate, William Cushing of Massachusetts, was ill.

According to those who heard them, all four advocates acquitted themselves brilliantly. They conducted one of the few great constitutional debates before the Supreme Court in which no pleader offered to tell the bench what the framers had in mind. Aside from the fact that it would have been impertinent, since some of the framers were on the bench, none of the notes on the proceedings at the Constitutional Convention of 1787 would be published until forty years later, so closely had the delegates guarded the secrecy of their debates.

Fortunately, the issue Hylton raised was fairly clear. Article I, Section 8 of the Constitution reads: "No Capitation, or other direct Tax shall be laid, unless in Proportion to the Census or Enumeration herein below directed to be taken."

Did that mean Congress could itself levy nothing except customs duties and fees? Or did "direct" apply only to poll taxes and land taxes? Hamilton cut through a great deal of the verbiage when he put it this way:

"The following are presumed to be the only direct taxes: Capitation or poll taxes; taxes on land and buildings; general assessments, whether on the whole property of individuals, or on their whole, real, or personal property. All else must of necessity be considered indirect taxes." He was not quite so clear when he tried to explain the grounds for his presumption.

As was the custom in these early sessions of the Court, each judge delivered his own opinion in reverse order of seniority, beginning with the newest, which was the English fashion. All four upheld the constitutionality of the tax; Daniel Hylton was out sixteen dollars, and the new government was delivered from what might have been crippling fiscal restrictions.

Chase started off by saying that if he had any doubts, he would accept the word of Congress that a carriage tax was more in the nature of a duty than a direct tax. But he had no doubt that only land and poll taxes were direct, and so the law was valid.

Paterson also was certain the framers meant this by direct tax, "principally . . . I will not say only." He went at some length into the question of whether a tax on the yield of land, such as rent, might be a direct tax, since land has no other value than its produce. He spent even more time ridiculing the whole apportionment idea. He said—and he should have known because he was there—that the provision was inserted solely to prevent a tax on slaves. Lashing out at the compromise that these people were included in the count on which representation in the House was based, he asked: "Why should slaves, who are a species of property, be represented any more than other property?" He recalled the exclusion of land taxes as due to a fear that such levies would be unfair to large, sparsely populated states as compared to small, thickly settled ones, since the tax would have to be so much an acre. He concluded by quoting Adam Smith's *Wealth of Nations* that a "coach tax" is a sort of license fee for using luxuries—reference to the social sciences was not invented by the Warren Court in the 1950s, as some commentators seem to think.

Iredell thought that the Constitution meant by direct taxes only those that could be apportioned according to population, such as a head tax. A carriage tax could not be fairly collected on that basis. By population, he said, Virginians might have to pay only three dollars a vehicle to raise their share, while in Connecticut the fee might be thirty-five dollars. Iredell found that for this reason if for no other the act under review was constitutional.

Wilson noted that he had been one of the judges who originally heard the case in Virginia. He had then been of the opinion that the act was constitutional, and he remained of that opinion. He did not attempt to say what he and his colleagues in the Constitutional Convention nine years before had in mind when they agreed upon the taxation clause.

On the strength of the fiscal philosophy established by *Hylton v. U.S.*, Congress levied quite a wide variety of taxes during the next ninety-nine years. Several times between 1797 and 1817 a direct tax on land, dwellings, and slaves was apportioned among the states. But from then until just before the Civil War, the Federal Government subsisted, and sometimes ran a surplus, on customs revenues, postal receipts, and the sale of public lands, with not even a single excise tax.

The exigencies of the war led to almost all varieties of taxation now known, including an inheritance tax and an income tax with only $800 and later $600 exempted. This tax was reduced after the war and abolished in 1872. By 1883 most of the other war taxes were dropped, too, except for the customs and excises on liquor and tobacco. The Government really needed no more money than it got from these sources, but the income tax issue became involved in the battle over protective tariffs. Farmers, workers, and consumers began to agitate for an income tax to prevent the protectionist forces from increasing customs duties as a revenue measure. A Supreme Court decision in 1880 encouraged the idea, for it upheld in retrospect the Civil War income tax on the ground that only land and poll taxes were "direct" under the Constitution.

The 1880 Court had been hearing the appeal of William M. Springer of Springfield, Illinois, to prevent the internal revenue department from evicting him from land it claimed for non-payment of his 1864 income tax. Springer, a successful lawyer, had been assessed $4,799.80 on an income of $50,798. He refused to pay on the ground that the law of 1864 unconstitutionally levied a direct tax, whereupon the tax collector ordered city lots that Springer owned sold to meet the bill. The Government was also the purchaser, and it sued Springer to evict him.

An Illinois jury handed down a verdict against Springer, who thereupon took his case to the October term of the Supreme Court. He argued it himself but convinced no members of the Court. Swayne wrote for all of them that surely this had been settled in 1796. The justice quoted the opinions then delivered, Hamilton's brief, a remark by Chief Justice Salmon P. Chase in a more recent decision that "in the practical construction of the Constitution" only land and poll taxes are direct, and finally a passage from the illustrious Chancellor Kent to the same effect.

"We are not aware that any writer, since *Hylton v. United States* was decided, has expressed a view of the subject different from these authors," Swayne asserted.

Congress's taxing power seemed secure enough if the Government should ever need it, and in the session of 1894, the combination of a Federal deficit after the panic of '93, a Western and Southern majority in the House, and a Democrat, Grover Cleveland, in the White House led to adoption of a new income tax. As signed on August 19, the measure assessed all personal and corporate incomes at a flat 2 percent after the first $4,000. This was strictly a "soak the rich" device. Only a small fraction of the people earned $4,000 a year. A dollar a day was still a fair wage for unskilled workers. The year the Supreme Court took up the income tax cases, an honor graduate of M.I.T.'s first class of electrical engineers received twelve and a half cents an hour on his first job in a Western Electric plant in Chicago. He got along quite well, although he worked the relatively new, shortened, fifty-six-hour week. The manager of his department was paid $2,500 a year. Such workers were as well off as their counterparts had been a generation or two earlier, but some of them viewed with indignation the amassing of fortunes greater than had ever been known before by new masters of the market place. The law of 1894 was as much a concession to their feelings as a response to Government needs.

In 1895, the second of two deficit years saw Federal expenditures rise to a staggering $356,195,000, largest since the Civil War, against only $324,729,000 in receipts. Much of this last still came from the sale of public lands—the per capita taxes paid to their government by Americans was a little more than $2, very little of it by anyone earning as much as $4,000 a year. The average annual wage of workers in all occupations was $411, ranging from the bituminous coal miner's $282 to a Federal employee's $1,084. This was the year that saw the first automobile manufactured for sale, the first moving picture shown on a screen, the first cafeteria, the first open golf tournament, and the first professional football game. This year, too, the National Association of Manufacturers was formed and electric power was transmitted from Niagara Falls, initially for the reduction of aluminum, a metal that had been produced commercially for only ten years. Politicians were preparing for the first million-dollar Presidential campaign on record; the Republicans in 1896 spent an estimated ten to fifteen millions to elect William McKinley over the silver crusader, William Jennings Bryan.

The legal test of the outrage against the accumulators of great wealth, so some of the accumulators regarded it, was almost as spurious as *Hylton v. U.S.* Congress had provided that "no suit for the purpose of restraining the assessment or collection of any tax shall be maintained in any court." This attempt to bar an attack on the income tax was frustrated by eminent counsel retained on behalf of Charles Pollock, a Massachusetts stockholder of the Farmers' Loan and Trust Co. of New York. These ingenious gentlemen noted that Congress did not forbid lawsuits to restrain people from paying the tax. They brought an action against the trust company on behalf of Pollock and all the other stockholders to prevent it from paying the tax on its own income or on that of any of the trusts for which it acted. Pollock lost in the circuit court for the Southern District of New York, and appealed.

While counsel for the company and others facing similar suits submitted briefs, Attorney General Richard Olney delivered the main argument for the constitutionality of the income tax. He had as high an idea of the authority of the Federal Government as one could find. The year before, he had obtained an injunction against the massive Pullman strike and sent Eugene V. Debs to jail. Later in 1895, Cleveland promoted him to Secretary of State, from which post he proclaimed the United States as "virtually sovereign on this continent," a sentiment his successors have never been able to eradicate from the minds of other American nations. In the first full five days of debate before the Court between March 7 and 18, 1895, he assured the judges that the impressive array of legal talent arrayed against him was there only to help the rich avoid paying taxes. The whole case, he said, "is nothing but a call upon the judicial department of the Government to supplant the political in the exercise of the taxing power."

Joseph Choate, replying for Pollock, was one of the most successful advocates of his entire half century at the bar. He developed the line that the *Hylton* precedent stemmed entirely from Hamilton's flat statement about direct and indirect taxes. This actually was founded on no evidence at all, Choate asserted. No one wanted to tell Congress how to levy taxes, he assured the Court, except to be sure the methods were sanctioned by the Constitution.

A number of other lawyers had their say, too, and when the eight judges who had heard them—one was ill—retired to their conference, they were as badly divided as any group since the legal tender hassle. Justice Field was the only holdover from that time. Chief Justice Melville W. Fuller had been appointed by Cleveland from Chicago, where he had been an important figure in Democratic politics. John Marshall Harlan of Kentucky, a slaveholder before the Civil War, a Union Colonel during it and a conservative Republican afterward, was supposed to owe his elevation to the Supreme Court in 1877 to his exertions on behalf of President Hayes's nomination in 1876. By 1895, Harlan had made a reputation as a great dissenter and the Court's leading champion of civil rights. David Brewer of Kansas, who was Field's nephew; Henry Billings Brown of Michigan; and Horace Gray, former Chief Justice of Massachusetts, were regarded as the workhorses of the Court. Recent members were George Shiras of Pittsburgh and Howell E. Jackson of Tennessee, named by Harrison shortly before leaving office in 1893. Newest of all was Edward Douglass White, former Confederate cavalryman who had been serving as Senator from Louisiana when Cleveland picked him for the bench just a year before.

Differences of opinion were so wide and deep that the judges needed two sets of opinions to settle all the issues. The first set was read on April 8, 1895. By 6 to 2, the Court ruled out as unconstitutional a Federal tax on the income from land. Unanimously, it held that income from municipal bonds was beyond the reach of

Congress, too. On all the other questions—was the tax sufficiently uniform? Was income from personal property taxable? Should any of the act be salvaged if part was killed?—the split was 4 to 4. So, at the suggestion of counsel, Fuller set reargument for May 6, 7, and 8, when the ailing Justice, Jackson, would return, but stipulated that each side confine itself to five hours of talk.

After this hearing, another judicial conference produced a bare majority to nullify the rest of the act of 1894. Field, Gray, Brewer, and Shiras joined Fuller, who delivered the opinion of the Court on May 20. Harlan, Jackson, White, and Brown filed separate dissents. Shiras had changed his mind between the two decisions.

The essence of Fuller's reversal of *Hylton* was that many taxes other than land and poll taxes are direct, and it was time to recognize the plain meaning of words. The Chief Justice went into a good deal more of the history of the Constitutional Convention than had been thought necessary ninety-nine years before. He wanted to prove that the framers were chary of giving too much power to Congress. Then he quoted from the 1876 opinions of Chase, Paterson, and Iredell to support his thesis that they had not positively ruled out a tax on rents as a direct tax. He saw the interpretation given to *Hylton* in *Springer* as founded on error. He reminded those who liked to lean on English precedents that income taxes "have always been classed by the law of Great Britain as direct taxes."

None of the judges, it appeared, including Fuller, wished to apply that definition in this country. The only point on which the nine agreed was that the Constitution permitted the Federal Government to tax income from professions, trades, and employment. For a short time, between the dates of the two sets of opinions, it appeared that this section of the 1894 tax might be permitted to stand. But by 5 to 4, the Court decided to throw out the entire law, as Field had wanted to do from the first. Fuller explained that if only salaries, wages, and professional fees were taxed, the burden would fall where Congress never meant to place it, that "what was intended as a tax on capital would remain in substance a tax on occupations and labor."

The dissents were vigorous and presented *in extenso*. Harlan's alone ran to forty-seven printed pages. He and Field, the two survivors of the 1880 Court, had concurred in *Springer*, and Harlan was of the same opinion still. White, who said the Court should have refused to consider the case at all because it was a suit to restrain the collection of a tax in fact, added that he deemed it unnecessary to elaborate his reasons for disagreeing with the majority. He then gave those reasons in twenty-one long, numbered paragraphs. Brown called the ruling "a strange commentary upon the Constitution of the United States and upon a democratic government that Congress has no power to lay a tax which is one of the main sources of revenue for nearly every civilized State." Jackson labeled the outcome "the most disastrous blow ever struck at the constitutional power of Congress."

The country took eighteen years to follow one bit of advice in Fuller's opinion. He suggested that if a Federal income tax was as necessary as the dissenters said, a constitutional amendment could end all argument. This method of overruling the Court is a little slow, of course, but in 1913, when White was Chief Justice and the only member left from 1895, the Sixteenth Amendment conferred upon Congress power to tax incomes "from whatever source derived."

✑ 7 ✑

Into the Twentieth Century

The Supreme Court narrowly escaped an unpalatable choice between standing by its income tax decision and executing another about-face. Congressmen holding the old Jeffersonian and Jacksonian view that the legislative and executive branches of government are as fit to interpret the Constitution as the judicial branch pushed hard for an only slightly modified income tax law that would force a new test case. This proposal gained strength when it was learned that if Justice Jackson had been present for the April decision, the Court would have upheld the act. Shiras had voted that way, joining Harlan, White, and Brown. A few weeks later, he changed his mind, praised by some for a courageous, wholesome willingness to reconsider possible error and denounced by others for shameful instability.

An income tax was introduced after Taft became President in 1909 with the avowed purpose of forcing Supreme Court reconsideration. The sponsors were confident that the current judges would agree with the large body of opinion that held the 1895 decision wrong, especially as the vote had been so close and had, as one senatorial debater put it, "itself overruled the decisions of a hundred years." The measure was defeated, partly by Presidential influence and persuasion. Taft conceded that the Court had been mistaken in 1895, but he preferred the slower amending process, saying:

"For the Congress to assume that the Court will reverse itself, and to enact legislation on such an assumption, will not strengthen popular confidence in the stability of judicial construction of the Constitution. It is much wiser policy to accept the decision and remedy the defect by amendment in due and regular course."

The twenty years between the passage of the 1894 income tax and the outbreak of World War I saw greater social and technological changes than had been known in the preceding century. Electrification of the cities, the rise of the automobile and motion picture, mass production, the first airplanes, the birth control movement, transformation from a predominantly rural to predominantly urban population, and the winning surge toward woman's suffrage all took place in this era. Einstein had evolved the theory of relativity and studied the motion of atoms by 1909. Freud's theories had won public recognition if not understanding. Marconi's wireless was in common use. Railroads had reached their peak of expansion—1902 was the only year in history in which more than six thousand miles of track were laid, and 1916 was the last for as much as one thousand miles.

The years between the income tax cases and the outbreak of World War I were not prolific of about-faces in the Court. Rather, the bench over which Fuller presided until 1910, when White succeeded him, handed down a good many decisions in key areas of national development that were to be overruled later. Some antedated the income tax and all were characteristic of the era when the Court was in tune with the country's mood for progress under the very slightly regulated leadership of its enterprising businessmen. Such countercurrents as reform movements generated were unavailing against the rise of the United States to industrial preeminence among the nations of the world, the expansion resulting from the war with Spain, and the final passing of the frontier. The Supreme Court reflected the majority, and it is perhaps significant that the last justice appointed by a Democratic President was Rufus W. Peckham of New York, who succeeded Jackson, dead within three months of his share in the income tax decision.

The decision of this Court that became the first to be. overruled extended the "due process" clause to a degree that was considered by many even at the time to lean over backward to protect criminals. The case came up in 1896 from the Western District of Arkansas, where Alex W. Crain had been convicted of forgery and sentenced to three years at hard labor in the House of Correction in Detroit. From his prison, he raised a highly technical point in the hope of winning a new trial.

Crain had been found guilty of a pension fraud against the United States. On August 4, 1892, he had forwarded to the Commissioner of Pensions a certificate declaring that an Indian named Spahiga, a resident of the Creek Nation, Indian Territory, had enlisted in 1863 in Company D First Regiment, Indian Home Guards, for service in the War of the Rebellion. The names Pahose Marell and Nokos Fixoco appeared as witnesses, and Crain signed the certificate as "U.S. Comm'r, Pension Notary." A Federal grand jury indicted him as having forged the claim, and when he appeared in district court with his lawyer, the judge tried the case at once.

Neither Crain nor his lawyer objected to this brisk procedure at the time, but after sentence had been passed they decided that his rights had been infringed. They said he had not been arraigned formally so that he could plead to the indictment, and so had not had a fair trial.

The Supreme Court, 6 to 3, ordered the district to conduct the case properly with an arraignment before trial. Justice Harlan, who spoke for the majority, called this "a matter of substance." He noted that the law required a plea be entered before trial, and arraignment is an essential step in entering a plea. Harlan had ample historical background for his contention, and he quoted Sir Matthew Hale, who more than three hundred years earlier had set down the exact wording of the entire procedure with appropriate statements for all concerned, right up to the reply of an accused when asked how he wished to be tried: "By God and my country."

While Harlan did not indicate that such precision was part of American law, he and his five colleagues regarded the arraignment as an indispensable element of due process.

Peckham, the new man on the Court, wrote a dissent in which Brewer and White joined—not the first time Brewer had confounded critics who had feared he would be a mere echo of his uncle, a member of the majority in this case. The minority had held that a merely technical objection not mentioned until the appeal was heard should not invalidate an otherwise orderly proceeding. They were willing to "presume" an arraignment and plea of not guilty since the only presumption to which the accused is entitled is the presumption of his innocence. Peckham added that from the state of the record it appeared the clerk simply failed to note the arraignment and plea. But even if it was not mere inadvertence, it was of no consequence and no substance. In Hale's time, Peckham pointed out, such technicalities were one of the accused's few safeguards from severe and often cruel punishment, for he was not represented by counsel and seldom could obtain witnesses for his defense.

Eighteen years later, the Court decided that Peckham's had been "the better opinion when applied to a situation such as now confronts us," the phrase of Justice William R. Day, who wrote for a unanimous Court in 1914. He quoted from Peckham freely—justices take pains to explain their minority views partly because today's dissent may become the foundation for tomorrow's about-face. White, who had shared Peckham's views, had not changed his mind and now concurred in overruling the majority decision of 1896. Others agreeing were Oliver Wendell Holmes and Charles Evans Hughes.

The appellant, a man named Garland, already had been the beneficiary of one new trial granted on narrow, technical grounds in King County, Utah. There he had been convicted of the larceny of one thousand dollars "lawful money." He won his second trial on the ground that his offense had been improperly described. The information was amended to accuse him of the larceny of "a check payable for the sum of one thousand dollars in money." Again convicted, he came to the Supreme Court to ask still another trial because he had not been arraigned before the second trial. *Crain v. U.S.* seemed to guarantee him that privilege as due process under the Fourteenth Amendment. The State rejected the idea, affirming the conviction. In taking the same view, Justice Day explained:

> Due process of law, this Court has held, does not bind the states to adopt any particular form of procedure, so long as it appears that the accused has had sufficient notice of the accusation and adequate opportunity to defend himself.

Garland certainly had the necessary opportunity and knew as well as anyone could have told him at an arraignment the nature of the case against him.

"Technical objections of this character were undoubtedly given much more weight formerly than they are now," Day conceded,

and went on to repeat much of Peckham's explanation for
scrupulously observing them when they were the accused's main
defense against barbarous penalties. Then, to make sure no one
would think he was applying the new rule only to state courts and
not federal courts, Day added: "Holding this view, notwithstand-
ing our reluctance to overrule former decisions of this Court, we
now are constrained to hold that the technical enforcement of
formal rights in criminal procedure sustained in the *Crain Case* in
and so far as that case is not in accordance with the views herein
expressed is necessarily overruled."

The White Court reversed two other decisions in the field of
crime, one of them striking down a highly technical rule that had
been honored, although sometimes in the breach, since Chief
Justice Taney enunciated it in 1851. His authority was the
Judiciary Act of 1789. He deduced his principle from language the
Congress had not changed since then, and had not changed when
the Supreme Court construed it again after a lapse of nearly 130
years from the original statement.

The problem began when Thomas Reid and Edward Clements
were brought to trial in a United States court in Virginia on a
charge of murder. It was a Federal case because the crime had
occurred on an American ship at sea. The men were tried sepa-
rately at their own request, Reid first. When his defense called
Clements as a witness, the prosecutor objected. The judge ruled
that one man indicted for the same crime could not testify in the
case of the other. Reid was convicted, and appealed on the ground
that his rights had been fatally infringed when the jury was not
allowed to hear Clements. The circuit court for Virginia could not
agree on the justice of this denial, and so the Supreme Court in
1851 heard the case.

Taney examined meticulously the development of rules of
evidence in Federal courts conducting criminal trials. The general
principle was that the United States judges adopted the rules of the
state in which they operated or the state of which the accused was
a resident. This rested on the Judiciary Act of 1789, which if it had

simply enjoined following the rules of the state would have been clear. But the act was not so specific. In fact, it said nothing about who might or might not testify. The Court had to look for relevant implications in other provisions. Taney thought he found one in a stipulation that qualifications for jurors in Federal trials and methods of selecting them should be those of the state at the time the act of 1789 went into effect. Taney deduced that Congress intended rules governing the trial to be those of the state, too, except as Congress might change them. In 1789, Virginia law excluded the testimony of a witness accused of the same crime as the defendant, although that no longer was the case. Taney noted that the practice he now approved had been followed in United States courts for sixty years, and should continue until Congress gave a contrary direction.

"But no law of a State made after 1789 can affect the mode of procedure or the rules of evidence in criminal cases, and the testimony of Clements was therefore properly rejected," Taney concluded.

While the pre-1789 rules of evidence were not uniformly or invariably followed in all Federal trials, *Reid* remained in effect until *Rosen* et al. *v. U.S.*, and *Pakas v. U.S.* turned up on the December 1917 docket of the Supreme Court. Three convicted felons wanted to have their convictions reversed because the judge of the Eastern District of New York declined to follow a rule that had been in effect there in 1789. One Broder, who had once served a term for forgery, testified that he had been in partnership with Rosen and another accomplice, Wagner, to receive letters and checks stolen from individual letter boxes in office and apartment buildings, and with Pakas for the same purpose. The reason his testimony must be stricken, the three maintained, was that under the common law of New York in 1789 a convicted forger was incompetent to be a witness in any trial unless or until he was pardoned. Broder had only been released at the expiration of his sentence.

Justices Willis Van Devanter, a Taft appointee from Wyoming, and James C. McReynolds, said to have been named as Wilson's first appointment to get him out of the Cabinet, where he had been Attorney General, held that the *Reid* precedent should be followed. Justice John H. Clarke of Ohio, Wilson's latest and last appointee, wrote for the rest of the Court that the tendency in trials now was to let jurors judge a witness's credibility. He conceded that *Reid* had never been specifically overruled, but "its authority must be regarded as seriously shaken." Whereupon he struck it down completely by deciding that the district court had properly admitted Broder's testimony and the convictions should stand.

The same nine judges who heard this appeal also overruled, and unanimously, a much more recent decision in a criminal case, although four of them had concurred in the earlier ruling, *Matter of Heff*. The crime alleged had been selling liquor to an Indian.

The United States District Court for Kansas in 1904 had sentenced Heff to four months in prison and fined him $200 and costs for selling to John Butler, a Kickapoo, "certain malt, spiritous, and vinous liquors . . . to wit, two quarts of beer, more or less." Heff did not dispute the sale but he contended that the act of Congress of 1897 prescribing the penalty was unconstitutional when applied to Butler because the Kickapoo had become a citizen, thereby ceasing to be a ward of the United States to whom liquor might not be sold.

Butler acquired his new status under a law of 1887. The Government allotted him a tract of land which it held in trust for him for twenty-five years and would then convey to him with no strings attached. Upon "allotting and patenting" the land Congress had provided, an Indian should have the benefits and obligations of citizenship. During the trusteeship period, he was to be considered a member of his tribe. The question at issue was the date on which Congress intended Indians to become citizens. Did they have to wait twenty-five years, or did they gain citizenship and all their new privileges when the allotment was made?

Justice Brewer answered for the Court. He delivered a learned discourse on the Government's relations with the Indians through the long era of treaties up to 1871 when Congress decreed that no tribe or people would be recognized as a nation to be dealt with by treaty. Since then, the subjection of the Indians to United States authority had been affirmed often. But, Brewer pointed out, in recent years a new policy was instituted to settle Indians in individual homes on their own land rather than on communal reservations. They were to be free from national guardianship and charged with "all the rights and obligations of citizens." Congress must have meant that to take effect at once, for it would not legislate in such detail twenty-five years ahead of time, the Court held. So Butler was an American and a Kansan, and no one could be penalized for selling him two quarts of beer. Justice Harlan dissented without saying why.

The District Court of South Dakota relied upon this decision when in 1914 it released a trader named Nice who had sold "whiskey and other intoxicating liquor" in Tripp County to a Sioux who is not identified. The Government appealed, and after hearing arguments in April 1916, the Supreme Court decided that the meaning of Congress had become clearer with the passage of a dozen years. While the new opinion's author, Justice Van Devanter, did not say so, the nation's attitude toward Indians was harsher than at the turn of the century. Many tribes had been pushed out of fertile lands to be resettled (after a good deal of violence) in barren, often malarial reservations. With the coming of the automobile, officialdom learned that some of the reservations were on extremely rich oil fields. White men presumptuously supposed Indians to be no more fit to have wealth than liquor, and desires to end their status as wards of the Government evaporated rapidly.

The Court reflected the new spirit. Although the Chief Justice and three associates—McKenna, Holmes, and Day—had concurred in the *Heff* opinion, they now joined in its overruling.

In justification, Justice Van Devanter recited the constitutional clause that empowered Congress to regulate commerce with the Indian tribes. This must mean, he said, commerce with individual members of the tribes. An Indian with an allotment, even if a citizen, retained his tribal relationship unless Congress specifically ended it. Also, only Congress by a specific act could end its guardianship. The laws, Van Devanter asserted, were always to be interpreted in the Indians' interest, which was not to sell them intoxicating liquor. He recognized that the Court had given a different construction to *Heff*, but that was before the intent of Congress had become clear, so now "we are constrained to hold that the decision in that case is not well grounded, and it is accordingly overruled."

The White Court did not confine its about-faces to criminal matters. Two examples, both falling entirely within the span of the Chief Justice's service on the Court, reveal how opinions change under the impact of a new entertainment industry, in this case the movies, and new patterns of life, those of commuting suburbanites. The case that involved the future of the motion picture also shows the not uncommon prescience of some judges, who divine the future consequences of a decision they oppose. Sometimes they live to take part in a majority opinion that vindicates them.

Inventions, being the children of necessity, have been the object of a great many custody actions ever since President Washington, Secretary of State Jefferson, and Attorney General Randolph put their signatures to the first patent in 1790. It was granted to Samuel Hopkins of Vermont for a process to make potash and pearl ashes. Lulls in the struggle have been deceptive. The head of the patent office wanted to quit in 1830 because, with some nine thousand patents already granted, obviously everything had been invented. More than three million patents later, we still have not solved some of the problems inherent in a system that tries to give the inventor full rights to his invention and the public its full benefits. In the early years of the twentieth century men like Charles Kettering for General Motors and Willis Whitney and Charles Steinmetz for General Electric were establishing great corporation research laboratories to make sure, as Kettering put it, that "today's dream is tomorrow's actuality." Law had something to say about the disposition of their findings, and the Supreme Court's pronouncements have greatly transcended the field of entertainment. Changes of the Court's mind have had more important effects on our uses and abuses of technology than is always immediately apparent.

In the early months of 1917, the Court was asked to legitimatize a stranglehold that the possessor of a key patent had fastened upon every producer and exhibitor of films in the country. The medium was no longer a cheap novelty but a serious challenge to the stage. Two years before, the first picture ever to win contemporary critical acclaim or open in a Broadway house at a two-dollar top, *The Birth of a Nation*, had confirmed the emergence of a new national institution. Already the industry was enormously profitable and clearly would become more so.

Jeremiah J. Kennedy, a retired engineer who had been placed at the head of a pioneer movie company, Biograph, to introduce business methods, saw how the profits might be concentrated. He organized eight other manufacturers and a distributor of films in the Motion Picture Patents Company. With the leverage of the patents they controlled, the group could monopolize the business by requiring all exhibitors to show only their films. Only their patented projector was capable of throwing a satisfactory image on the country's thousands of screens—forty thousand was one estimate. The trick was to sell the projectors fairly cheaply and make the big money on the sale or lease of films, which could not be patented but could be shown only with a patented machine.

The patent on which the company relied had been granted in 1902 to a Virginia college professor, Woodville Latham, for the mechanism that feeds film through a projector at an even speed without so strong a pull that it breaks the film. In 1912 the company licensed the Precision Machine Company to manufacture projectors on condition that none be used except for films from producers also licensed by Motion Picture Patents. Each machine was to carry a plate on which was set forth these terms and a further notice that removal or defacement of the plate terminated a buyer's right to use the projector. Precision agreed to sell the projectors for not more than $150 each—less to jobbers—plus a royalty.

Monopolies were then highly unpopular and the Sherman Anti-Trust Act was supposed to drive them from the marketplace. But bigger trusts than Motion Picture Patents had survived, and the company had one priceless constitutional protection not vouchsafed to many others, "securing for limited times to . . . inventors the exclusive right to their respective . . . discoveries." Furthermore, the Supreme Court had spelled out clearly what those words meant for the holders of a key patent as recently as 1912. The case was entitled *Henry v. A. B. Dick Company*, and the parallel with the Motion Picture Patents claim was as exact as legal precedents are likely to come.

Dick, an Illinois company, owned patents on a stencil duplicating machine new enough that the court used quotation marks in naming it "Rotary Mimeograph." The company sold one to Miss Christina B. Skou of New York City. Attached was a notice headed "License Restriction," which stipulated the purchaser's agreement to use only stencils, paper, and ink made by Dick.

Sidney Henry, a partner in a firm that carried another brand of ink, sold a can of it to Miss Skou, knowing of the agreement and expecting the ink to be used in the patented machine, according to the complaint.

That complaint was lodged in United States Court against Henry because any suit against Miss Skou could only have been for breach of contract. The company was more interested in enforcing its monopoly on supplies than in the machine itself. The district court held that this was the patent holder's privilege, and the circuit court of appeals granted an injunction to prevent Henry from trying to procure "any breach or violation of the covenant." But the judges posed for the Supreme Court a question they could not answer: "Did the acts of the defendant constitute contributory infringement of the complainants' patents?"

When counsel argued this point on October 27, 1911, only seven justices were listening. Harlan had died thirteen days before, after one of the most distinguished of judicial careers, and Justice Day was absent. Justice Horace Lurton, appointed the previous year when Fuller died and White became Chief Justice, delivered the Court's opinion that the patentee was within his rights in restricting a user to certain unpatented supplies. Surely, he said, an owner could choose to sell his patented machine at cost and make his profit from other items. In this instance, Dick was only monopolizing the market for ink that its mimeograph device had created; if the company had chosen to withhold the patent from use, which was its privilege, no ink would have been sold for the machine at all, so "he took nothing from others and in no wise restricted the legitimate market." The answer to the circuit court's question was affirmative and Henry must stop selling ink to owners of rotary mimeographs.

This seemed to authorize the Motion Picture Patents Company to force their films on all exhibitors. But only three associates, Holmes, McKenna, and Van Devanter, had concurred in Lurton's opinion. The Chief Justice dissented and was joined by Justices Joseph Lamar, appointed from Georgia the year before, and Charles Evans Hughes, former governor of New York, also named in 1910 after Brewer died. These three doubted that the Constitution had intended to give patent holders control over unpatentable items. They warned that this decision would affect everybody through all sorts of monopolies. They envisaged a sewing machine patentee with a monopoly on needles, thread, and fabrics or a maker of some new cooking utensil cornering a large segment of the food market. White, who wrote the dissent, said:

> My mind cannot shake off the dread of the vast extension of such practices which must come from the decision of the Court now rendered.

He thought the Constitution's phrase, "exclusive right to . . . discoveries" meant only that—the use of the device itself in ways for which it was patented. He believed the circuit court in enjoining Henry against trying to procure a breach of contract had in effect conceded that this was not a patent case at all but a contract case, and as such no business of the Federal courts.

White was the only member of this trio still on the Court when the motion picture case was argued six years later, in January 1917. Hughes had resigned the previous June to run for President, unsuccessfully, and Lamar died shortly after that. Lurton also had died, and the bench had been filled by the only three appointments Wilson made in his two full terms as President—McReynolds; Louis D. Brandeis, after one of the bitterest confirmation battles in history; and Clarke, an able judge who would resign after World War I to devote himself to the cause of peace. Day had returned to duty and Mahlon Pitney, former chancellor of New Jersey, had taken Harlan's seat shortly after the *Dick* decision. Holmes, McKenna, and Van Devanter of the 1912 majority remained.

The test case for the movie monopoly, filed March 15, 1915, in the Southern District of New York, was brought against one of the independent producers, Universal, which had supplied two films to a theater on New York City's 72nd Street operated by the Prague Amusement Company. Prague leased the premises and equipment from another company that had bought a Precision projector, complete with warning notice. The district court held that the restriction imposed was invalid, that the buyer had an implied license to use the machine for any film. The circuit court of appeals agreed, but on the strength of *Dick*, the loser appealed.

The newest man on the Supreme Court, Clarke, wrote for the majority that at least since an 1829 opinion by Story, "this Court has consistently held that the primary purpose of our patent laws is not the creation of private fortunes for the owners of the patents but is 'to promote the progress of science and the useful arts.' "

Clarke saw the present case as governed by two rules stemming from this principle. First, the scope of a patent is limited to the claims made for the invention, as a title to land is limited to the boundaries specified in the deed. This means that the protection offered has "nothing to do with the materials with which or on which the machine operates." Second, the patentee gets nothing from the law except protection against others making, using, or selling his devices without his consent. This means he must make his profit from the patent monopoly the law gives him, not from a monopoly in other goods that he uses the patent to create. The restrictions that Motion Picture Patents attempted to impose, said Clarke, were "a potential power for evil over an industry which must be recognized as an important element in the amusement life of the country." So the case was imbued with a public interest that justified judicial action.

Clarke also mentioned that since *Dick*, Congress had passed a law, "as if in response to that decision," forbidding the sale of a patented article on condition the purchaser use with it no product of a competitor of the patent owner. This law could not deprive a patentee of any rights the Constitution gave him, but it did show that the national policy was against the plaintiff in this action.

"It is obvious," Clarke concluded, "that the conclusions arrived at in this opinion are such that the decision in *Henry v. Dick Co.* . . . must be regarded as overruled."

The holdovers from the 1912 majority were not convinced. Holmes wrote for the three that the issue was simply one of property, the property right in a patent. He rejected Clarke's notion that movies were affected with a public interest in the legal sense. If the owner of a patented teapot could quite legally keep the pot from anyone who would not use his tea, as Holmes thought he could, this "film feeder" (the justice's phrase) was equally at liberty to make his own rules. He was consistent in his application of law to entertainment. A few years after this dissent, he freed organized baseball from the operations of the Sherman Anti-Trust Act, writing for a unanimous Court that this particular sport could not be called trade or commerce but "giving exhibitions . . . which are purely state affairs."

For all the respect due the Holmesian philosophy, and whatever our opinion of the commercial cinematic output of the more than half a century since he spoke, we may be grateful that *Motion Picture Patents Co. v. Universal Film Manufacturing Co.* et al. overruled *Henry v. Dick Co.* It is not so clear that the same Court was as perceptive in the matter of commuter trains as in the future of the movies. Opinions on that point will differ with views of present-day suburbs and the railroads that serve them.

A few days after the motion picture decision and during the first weeks of our participation in World War I, the Court was called upon to review an 1899 decision in which the only two survivors, White and McKenna, had taken opposite sides. In 1899 commuters were an insignificant fraction of any city's work force, but such as they were they came and went on rails. By then states no longer left rate fixing to the forbearance of the carriers, and the right to establish a maximum charge per mile was no longer contested. In 1891, Michigan had added to its three cents a mile rate a provision for 1,000-mile tickets, good for a year, to be sold for twenty dollars in the Lower Peninsula and twenty-five dollars in the Upper. The tickets were nontransferable, but the purchaser's wife and children were entitled to ride on them. At the expiration date, the ticket holder could get a refund by paying three cents a mile for the portion used if that was to his advantage. Railroads ignored the law. Henry C. Smith, an Adrian, Michigan, lawyer, sued after twice failing to buy a 1,000-mile ticket on the Lake Shore and Southern Michigan Railroad. He eventually won in the state supreme court, and the railway company appealed.

The United States Supreme Court found for the company. A maximum rate or even a reduced fare, as during certain hours of the day, could be imposed if it applied to all, Justice Peckham wrote for the majority. But a lower rate for a favored segment of passengers amounted to taking the railroad's property in violation of the Fourteenth Amendment's due process clause. Chief Justice Fuller and Justices Gray and McKenna dissented without saying why.

This limitation on state authority held up until a combination of popular revulsion against the preponderant railroad influence in many sectors of the economy and a substantial rise in the number and importance of metropolitan "bedroom" communities brought the problem once more to the Supreme Court's attention. While a few daring souls were driving in and out of the city every day in some of the more than two million automobiles the country boasted when this suit was filed, neither roads nor cars were very reliable for steady commuting. The Interstate Commerce Commission had said in one of its rulings, favorably mentioned by the Court, that the prosperity and growth of the suburbs depended upon an efficient, reasonable rail service.

"Many such communities," the Commission added, "have not only been encouraged by the carriers, but were, in fact, originally established largely on their initiative. Suburban property has been bought, homes have been established, business relations made, and the entire course of life of many families adjusted to the conditions created by a commutation service."

Nevertheless, the Pennsylvania Railroad, for one, put its faith in the 1899 decision and the sanctity of due process to upset an order by the Public Service Commission of Maryland modifying commutation rates the railroad wanted to put into effect at the end of 1914 on a suburban line from Baltimore to Parkton. The Commission had accepted some, annulled others, and reduced the rest. Typical was the proposed ten-ride ticket. The old one, good for a year, was sold at 1.8 cents a mile. The road wanted 2½ cents and a three-months limit. The Commission agreed to three months but lowered the fare to 2¼ cents. Losing a lawsuit in the Maryland Court of Appeals, the Pennsylvania sought redress in the Supreme Court, pointing out that the reduction of a quarter of a cent a mile was clearly deprivation of property without due process.

The eighteen years between the middle of William McKinley's first term and the beginning of Woodrow Wilson's second witnessed more profound changes in American thinking and society than any equal period in previous history except possibly that of the Civil War and Reconstruction. The first Roosevelt's trust-busting, reinforcement of the Sherman Act, and immunity of labor from anti-trust provisions had enraged the men who considered big business the best bulwark of prosperity. The creation of such new agencies as the Food and Drug Administration, Federal Trade Commission, and Federal Reserve denoted a new public attitude toward the power of money. Government was getting bigger, and the war was making it even more expensive than most people had thought possible. Not only was the 1917 budget the first to top a billion dollars, but in three years, 1917–1919, Federal expenditures would exceed the total cost of government, including all previous wars, from the beginning in 1789 through 1916. Even before the United States entered the war, the Federal Treasury was taxing at the rate of $7.83 per capita, more than three times as much as in McKinley's day.

Lawyers for the company argued that ever since *Lake Shore* the state's regulating power extended only to setting the price of a single one-way ticket. Other, lower rates were completely at the discretion of the carrier. But by 6 to 3, the Supreme Court upheld the Commission. Justice Day for the majority could see no reason why a state with authority to fix a single fare could not determine the fair rate for multiples, especially when the railroad had already introduced commutation. He confessed that the Court was influenced by the great growth of suburbs relying upon special transportation rates. The Pennsylvania's right to due process of law had not been violated by the Commission's proceedings.

"True it is," Day admitted, "that it may not be possible to reconcile these views with all that is said in the opinion delivered for the majority of the Court in the case of *Lake Shore & Michigan Southern Ry. Co. v. Smith*. The views therein presented which are inconsistent with the right of the states to fix reasonable commutation fares, when the carrier has itself established fares for such services, must be regarded as overruled."

It is not surprising that White had not changed his mind on an issue that he had helped decide in 1899, so he dissented from the about-face. McReynolds joined him, for he was a great upholder of due process for corporations. But the dissent of McKenna is a little harder to understand, especially as none of the dissenters offered reasons. McKenna had dissented in *Lake Shore*, too, and was not usually so committed to *stare decisis* that he would not accept Court approval of his own views. At seventy-four, McKenna was not beyond the age of vigorous service on the Court—many judges have officiated with undiminished vitality far longer—but he was showing signs of the incapacity that in a few years led his colleagues to agree that if any case hinged on his vote they would not decide it.

❦ 8 ❦

The Case of People Versus Property

The 1897–1898 term of the Supreme Court, which set several of the overruled precedents already described, touched off one series of important decisions that seemed even to some of the judges intolerably vacillating. However, they eventually settled the authority of the state to prescribe maximum hours of labor and minimum wages for that labor. Meantime, in a span of forty years, the Court twice departed from and twice returned to its original opinion, which turned out to be the one the country needed and wanted. All five decisions were by divided Courts, which took a number of minor zigs and zags in between.

The confusion stemmed largely from the almost irresistible

power of an idea that gets blocked or stuck. Here the idea was that under the due process clauses of the Fifth and Fourteenth Amendments, state and Federal agencies are powerless to prevent men, women, or children from agreeing to work as long hours as an employer can persuade them to for as little as they will accept. Some of the decisions give the impression that the Court, in pursuit of this ideal, set one law above the Constitution, the law of supply and demand.

"Due process of law" does not mean to lawyers what the dictionary definitions of the words suggest. The dictionary would support the assumption that a determination on wages, hours, or utility rates reached by a government commission after hearings in accordance with a properly enacted statute is due process of law. But in law itself the phrase has a much vaguer meaning. It came into American jurisprudence from the British, first as a restriction on procedures and then developing into a requirement that governments must conform to the general principles that have been worked out to protect the people's rights and liberties.

Before the Civil War, and of course before the Fourteenth Amendment of 1868, the due process clause applied solely to the Federal Government. The Supreme Court used it only once to invalidate a statute, the Dred Scott decision of unhappy memory. Shortly after the adoption of the Fourteenth Amendment, which imposed due process upon the states, Justice Miller expressed doubt that it ever would be considered to cover any action not directed against Negroes as a class or race.

Exactly what general principles due process embodies cannot be stated precisely in language satisfactory to lawyers generally. So this part of the Constitution is truly what the judges say it is, as Hughes said of the whole document. But also, as Hughes went on in words that usually are omitted from the quotation, "and the judiciary is the safeguard of our liberty and of our property under the Constitution." Judges on the same Court very often disagree in their application of this principle, and successive Courts reach different conclusions from virtually the same evidence. While contradictions are characteristic of our system of law, due process seems to bring them out more than most passages the Supreme Court is called upon to interpret. If law remained completely static, we would need no such shifts. But law must remain flexible enough to adapt its rules to the changing realities in this world, and due process is a medium for transition from one set of legal principles to another.

Labor law illustrates this. In the 1890s, it had passed little beyond that governing the medieval guilds, although these had disappeared. The mostly ineffective associations of skilled workers had only recently been without any legal protection at all. The American Federation of Labor, made up of craft unions and led for its first thirty-eight years by Samuel Gompers of the cigar makers, one of the more powerful groups, had been formed in 1886 and ten years later had fewer than half a million members. The unskilled were not organized at all, and urban sweat shops had replaced rural cottage labor.

Legal restrictions on how long people could work were few. In 1868 Congress set eight hours for "all laborers, workers, and mechanics who may be employed by or on behalf of the Government of the United States." Ohio in 1852 had a law limiting hours of work for women and children to ten a day but repealed it in 1887. Beginning with Massachusetts in 1842, several states provided that children under twelve might not work more than ten hours a day. The census of 1900 showed that 1,750,178 children between ten and fifteen were "gainfully employed"—many got as little as twenty-five cents a day. They constituted more than 6 percent of the entire labor force of the country.

Hardly anyone could even dream of a future in which the workers might be masters in some industries rather than their employees, and law would be needed to curb the power of Gompers' successors. At the same time, the weak but sometimes vocal labor leaders were attracting a certain sympathy, and their followers had votes.

By the time of the 1896 election, when William McKinley saved the country from the silver heresy of William Jennings Bryan, legislators were discovering the difference in bargaining power between worker and boss. To compensate, they passed laws to regulate hours and wages. One of the first came up to the Supreme Court in 1897 from Utah, where the state's highest court had upheld a statute that limited work in underground mines, smelters, and metal refining plants to what was then an incredibly low eight hours a day, "except in cases of emergency where life or property is in imminent danger." The Utah judges said this was within the police power of the state and therefore did not violate due process. They pointed out that the restriction applied only to a special class of workers laboring under "peculiar conditions" that had serious effects upon health and were more than commonly hazardous. The Supreme Court agreed, declaring with two dissenting voices, fewest for any of the leading wages-and-hours decisions of four decades:

> While this Court has held . . . that the police power cannot be put forward as an excuse for oppressive and unjust legislation, it may be lawfully resorted to for preserving the public health, safety, or morals, or the abatement of public nuisance, and a large discretion is necessarily vested in the legislature. . . . The legislature has also recognized, which the experience of the legislators in many states has corroborated, that the proprietors of these establishments and their operators do not stand upon an equality, and that their interests are, to a certain extent, conflicting. . . . The proprietors lay down the rules and the laborers are constrained to obey them. In such cases, self-respect is often an unsafe guide, and the legislature may properly interpose its authority.

Justice Brown, who spoke for the majority, based the decision on the inexorable rule of law's change as life changes, and added ". . . in view of the fact that from the day Magna Carta was signed to the present moment amendments to the structure of the law have been made with increasing frequency, it is impossible to suppose that they will not continue, and the law be forced to adapt itself to new conditions of society." The growth of the mining and metals industries, he went on, led to the state's need to protect its people in ways that had not been required in simpler times.

In February 1905, when a very similar problem was posed, Justices Holmes and Day had replaced Gray and Shiras, both of whom had been in the 1897 majority. But resistance to so-called reformers and liberals who thought the horrors of contemporary mills and mines might be mitigated by law was hardening among the higher elements of the Establishment. The attitude of these influential persons had been well put during a long and bloody coal strike in 1902 by George Baer, president of a railroad that was also one of the biggest anthracite operators in the country. In strongly rejecting a proposal to arbitrate the demand for better pay, he expressed the philosophy of most large employers of that era: "The rights and interests of the laboring man will be protected and cared for—not by the labor agitators, but by the Christian men to whom God in his infinite wisdom has given control of the property interests of the country. Pray earnestly that right may triumph, always remembering that the Lord God Omnipotent still reigns."

While such statements aroused an inevitable, hostile reaction, the sentiment was shared widely among judges, and the protagonists of an expanding interpretation of due process indicated that if God was on the side of the owners, surely the Constitution must be too. These jurists outnumbered on the Court those who defended the use of police power for economic and social regulation. The lines between the two schools of thought were drawn clearly in the two February days of 1905 when *Lochner v. New York* was argued. It was an appeal from that state's prestigious court of appeals, which had upheld a New York statute apparently modeled on that of Utah.

The men who made up the industrial and financial Establishment of the United States were a badly scared lot in 1905. This year the frankly revolutionary IWW was formed, and the year before, the Socialist Party held its first convention. But the Establishment was not giving anything away. When the Georgia legislature was considering a bill to forbid children under twelve to work in mills, a Bostonian who managed one of the biggest Southern mills rallied the forces that defeated the measure, pointing out that the owners had a gentlemen's agreement that no ten-year-old work more than sixty-six hours a week—seventy-two was par for their elders of eleven and twelve. As far as adults were concerned, plenty of new workers kept arriving to keep wages down and hours up. In 1905 immigration topped a million for the first time. This was also the year that Mrs. John Jacob Astor's four hundred fifty guests at a ball had a ten-course dinner, a nine-course midnight supper and a five-course pre-dawn snack, and counsel for a New York State investigating committee, Charles Evans Hughes, uncovered scandals that led to a new regulation of insurance companies, elevating Hughes successively to Governor, Justice, candidate for President, and Chief Justice.

The particular statute under consideration in *Lochner v. New York*, known for short as the Labor Law, provided that no one should be permitted to work in biscuit, bread, or cake bakeries or in confectionery establishments for more than sixty hours in one week or ten hours in one day. An employer who violated this law committed a misdemeanor and was to be punished accordingly. Lochner, a Utica baker, "wrongfully and unlawfully required and permitted" an employee to work more than sixty hours a week, according to a complaint filed in the Oneida County Court. Summoned before that tribunal, Lochner demanded his discharge because the offense alleged was not a crime. Overruled, he refused to plead to the charge. The judge ordered a plea of not guilty entered for him; the trial proceeded; he was convicted and told to mend his ways. Lochner did not change the hours of work at his bakery, and was arrested again. As a second offender, he was fined fifty dollars and ordered to jail until the fine was paid or he had served fifty days. He lost each of his appeals through the chain of state courts and now appeared before the Supreme Court to protest that the Labor Law of New York violated the Fourteenth Amendment.

His lawyers contended that the statute was discriminatory, denying a few employers the equal protection of the laws since it forbade no other employers to work their employees more than sixty hours a week. The legislature had not exercised police power properly because health was not an issue—"there is no danger to the employee in a first-class bakery."

New York's Attorney General retorted that indeed long night hours in a hot bakery were injurious to health, and he quoted both judicial and medical authorities. Therefore, especially in light of the 1897 Utah decision, the Labor Law was a proper exercise of legislative authority.

Eight weeks later the Court, split five to four, issued three opinions, one by Peckham for the majority and two dissents by Harlan and Holmes, with White and Day subscribing to Harlan's. Fuller and McKenna had changed their minds since 1897, and the majority went to some pains to spare them an outright about-face by saying that really the Utah case did not apply.

Peckham seemed horrified by the suggestion that the Constitution could be thought to impugn George Baer's version of the ordained relationship between master and man. The majority clearly were outraged by a statute they said tried to enjoin an employer from letting a laborer earn extra money by sticking at his job more than sixty hours a week. (No evidence appears in the record to show that Lochner did actually pay anyone for overtime.)

The Fourteenth Amendment, said Peckham, protects the

worker in his right to sell his labor as he chooses. The state's police power can restrict rights guaranteed under the Fourteenth only to prevent such things as violation of a lawful statute or the letting of property for immoral purposes.

"The limitation of the hours of labor does not come within the police power," the opinion stated flatly.

The New York law was held to differ from the Utah law in that no exceptions were permitted to meet emergencies and because its pretensions to be a health measure were not sufficiently well founded to justify overriding the individual's liberty to contract for his labor.

The New York Court of Appeals majority had found baking unhealthy; it tended to result in respiratory diseases. The Supreme Court majority asserted "no fair doubt that the trade of a baker, in and of itself, is not an unhealthy one to that degree which would authorize the legislature to interfere with the right to labor."

Peckham added that if the statute were upheld, the time might come when the state would even restrict the hours of bank clerks or law clerks. Expressing strong suspicion that New York never meant its Labor Law as a health law, the majority opinion is replete with such phrases as "illegal interference with the rights of individuals" and "mere meddlesome interference with the rights of the individual."

Harlan's dissent called the Utah case not only applicable but controlling. He quoted from a treatise on "diseases of the workers" to prove that the New York judges were right and his colleagues of the majority wrong about the health hazards of baking. He thought the Court had enlarged the scope of the Fourteenth far beyond the intent of the framers and would seriously cripple the states in legislating on matters best left to them.

Holmes, agreeing with everything Harlan wrote, added that the Labor Law was like many that interfered justifiably with the citizen's liberties. He mentioned specifically Sunday laws, usury laws, school laws, vaccination laws, prohibiting of lotteries, "and every state or municipal institution which takes his money for purposes thought desirable whether he likes it or not." Then, in a sentence often quoted when the Court is accused of following its economic prejudices, he commented:

"The Fourteenth Amendment does not enact Mr. Herbert Spencer's *Social Statics* [the bible of laissez-faire economists]."

The Court took a zig away from *Lochner* within three years, chiefly because a Boston lawyer named Louis D. Brandeis revolutionized the way of presenting Supreme Court cases involving large social constitutional questions. Oregon had passed a law restricting the hours of work for women outside the home (where they were limitless) to ten a day. The validity of this was questioned in an appeal of 1908, *Muller v. Oregon*.

Brandeis got the job to defend the law because the most sought-after pleader of his generation, Joseph H. Choate, a premature Women's Lib protagonist perhaps, had refused the assignment. He would not support the view that "a big husky Irishwoman should not work more than ten hours a day in a laundry if she and her employer so desired."

Brandeis looked carefully at Peckham's *Lochner* opinion and then prepared his brief to answer it. Up to that time, briefs confined themselves to legal precedents and statements of law. But Brandeis was on record as believing, "A judge is presumed to know the elements of law, but there is no presumption that he knows the facts." So his brief in this case consisted of 2 pages of legalities and 101 pages of facts drawn from a great number of authoritative reports and studies to show that long hours of work undermine a woman's health, safety, and morals.

The brief and the argument were so convincing that the *Lochner* majority decided women might be protected even if bakers were not. Speaking through Justice Brewer, the Court declared that woman's physical structure and functions "justified special legislation restricting or qualifying the conditions under which she should be permitted to toil." This opinion distinguished the case from *Lochner* rather than overruled it.

Thus encouraged, Oregon in 1913 decreed a ten-hour day for all industrial workers except watchmen and employees engaged in emergency repairs or meeting some other emergency endangering life or property. On payment of time and a half for the extra time, the employer could add another three hours. Health was not mentioned. The state supreme court upheld this statute when Superintendent Bunting of the Lakeview Flouring Mills kept one Hammersley on the job for thirteen hours a day but did not pay time and a half for the overtime.

He appealed his conviction to the Supreme Court where *Bunting v. Oregon* was argued in April 1916. Before the judges finished considering it, Hughes had resigned and Lamar died. The case was put down for reargument in January 1917, by which time Brandeis and Clarke had taken their seats. White, now Chief Justice, McKenna, Holmes, and Day were the only holdovers from 1905.

An argument for Bunting not offered in previous hours cases was that the time and a half, being more than the market value of labor, took the corporation's property without due process of law.

McKenna, who delivered the opinion of the Court, met this plea by saying the intent of the extra money was to deter the employer from working his help more than the ten hours currently sanctioned by custom in industry. As a deterrent, it was a matter of legislative judgment. As a penalty, it would have violated due process, he conceded.

Nowhere in the opinion is *Lochner* so much as mentioned, but Holmes for one assumed that it had been overruled. So, too, apparently, did White, Van Devanter, and McReynolds, who dissented although delivering no opinion.

Brandeis took no part in the proceedings, because as an advocate on one side of the issue in a number of cases besides *Muller v. Oregon* it would have been improper for him to vote.

Nevertheless, *Lochner* turned up alive and well, and *Bunting* and

Muller became casualties in 1923 when the Court ruled on *Adkins* et al., *Constituting the Minimum Wage Board of the District of Columbia v. Children's Hospital of the District of Columbia.*

War had indeed changed the whole world, and one curious change was a turn to the right that gave direction of national affairs to the spokesmen of commerce and industry. The United States had become the greatest industrial country in the world, but organized labor attained a peak membership of only 5 million in 1921, a total that was shrinking due to open shop drives and anti-labor injunctions issued by the courts. Radio was on its way to becoming a genuine mass medium. The Radio Corporation of America, founded as a business for transoceanic wireless service, was making nearly four times as much money from selling radio sets, and A.T. & T. in 1922 broadcast from its New York station the first commercial. An airplane flew nonstop from coast to coast in 1923, and President Harding died just before the worst scandals of his Administration broke. Material growth was very much the mark of progress, and the total value of all reproducible tangible assets in the country, which had been estimated at 4½ billion dollars in 1850 and 59 billion in 1900, was 233 billion in 1922.

A few weeks before the end of the war in 1918, Congress had passed a minimum wage law for women and children, applicable only in the Federal district. No opposition was voiced in the House, and only twelve Senators voted nay. Congress had recognized women as people by passing the Nineteenth Amendment allowing them to vote, which the states ratified in 1920.

The 1918 act established a board of three members representing employers, employees, and the public. This board, after hearings, was empowered to set for any given occupation a wage that would meet the cost of living. It had ordered such minimums as $16.50 a week for women employed where food was served, $15.50 in a printing plant and $15 in a laundry, except for beginners who need get only $9 in this last trade. (A nickel then bought a loaf of bread and one cent *The New York Times.*)

The law had been in effect for four years when the Children's Hospital, a private corporation employing a great many women and paying them less than the minimum, asked the district court of appeals to enjoin the board from enforcing its orders. On the first try, with a Supreme Court justice sitting in place of a regular member, this court refused the injunction by a vote of 2 to 1. When the absent circuit judge returned, the court ordered a rehearing, and by 2 to 1 granted the injunction.

By the time the Supreme Court heard the board's arguments, presented by Professor Felix Frankfurter of Harvard, Taft had succeeded White as Chief Justice. Day, Pitney, and Clarke had retired. The newer members of the Court, all appointed within the year, were George Sutherland, a staunchly conservative English-born former Senator from Utah who had managed Harding's "front porch" campaign for the Presidency and been accorded the rare distinction of confirmation the day of his nomination without reference to a committee; Pierce Butler, a Minnesota railroad lawyer of equal conservatism and the first justice born west of the Mississippi; and Edward T. Sanford, a Tennessean who had taken his seat just in time to hear the case. Brandeis again took no part.

To the frank amazement of Taft and Holmes, a bare majority of the Court turned its back on *Bunting, Muller,* and a whole library of state labor decisions to declare *Lochner* a controlling precedent. Sutherland expressed the opinion of the Court. He noted that the women employed at the hospital were "of full legal age and under no legal disabilities" that warranted interference with their freedom. He quoted Peckham's *Lochner* decision at some length, then pointed out that *Muller* and *Bunting* had concerned hours, not wages. Limiting the work span for women was proper "in respect of the maternal function, and also in the fact that historically woman has always been dependent upon man, who has established his control by superior physical strength." That inequality, Sutherland thought, had almost reached the vanishing point "in view of the great—not to say revolutionary—changes which have taken place [since *Bunting*] in the contractual, political, and civil status of women, culminating in the Nineteenth Amendment."

Sutherland felt that women's emancipation included the privilege of bargaining like a man for a living wage. The opinion professed puzzlement over the board's calculation that a woman employed where food is served needs $16.50 a week for decent subsistence but her sister starting work in a laundry can get along on $9. Furthermore, power to fix a minimum wage might very well be used to justify a maximum, too, and so for the main issue before the Court:

> The statute now under consideration is attacked upon the ground that it authorizes an unconstitutional interference with the freedom of contract included within the guarantees of the due process clause. . . . That the right to contract about one's affairs is a part of the liberty of the individual protected by this clause is settled by the decisions of this Court, and is no longer open to question. Within this liberty are contracts of employment of labor. In making such contracts, generally speaking, the parties have an equal right to obtain from each other the best terms they can as the result of private bargaining.

The Chief Justice in his dissent, in which Sanford joined, contradicted Sutherland's distinction between laws establishing maximum hours and laws requiring minimum wages. Both, said Taft, rest upon the same legal foundation, and that should not be *Lochner*.

"It is impossible for me to reconcile the *Bunting Case* and the *Lochner Case*," he said, "and I have always supposed that the *Lochner Case* was thus overruled *sub silentio*."

Holmes, entering his third decade on the Court and in the full vigor of his eighty-two years, added a few dissenting remarks of his own bearing the stamp of his particular approach to construing the Constitution. He repeated much of what he had said in his *Lochner* dissent, but the heart of his objection to the rule reached by his juniors—McKenna at eighty was the only member within fifteen years of Holmes's age—ran as follows:

> I confess that I do not understand the principle on which the power to fix a minimum for the wages of women can be denied by those who admit the power to fix a maximum for their hours of work. . . . *Muller v. Oregon*, I take it, is as good law today as it was in 1908. It will need more than the Nineteenth Amendment to convince me that there are no differences between men and women, or that legislation cannot take those differences into account. I should not hesitate to take them into account if I thought it necessary to sustain this act. . . . But after *Bunting v. Oregon* . . . I had supposed that it was not necessary, and that *Lochner v. New York* . . . would be allowed a deserved repose.

As the technological advances of the first third of the twentieth century accelerated through the 1920s, culminating in boom, bust, and gradual recovery, the Supreme Court changed much less than the country in the fourteen years after *Adkins*. The population, which passed 100 million during the period of World War I, added 25 million more by the middle '30s. The transition from what was regarded as a high plateau of permanent prosperity under Coolidge to the worst depression in history under Hoover set the stage for a struggle between Roosevelt's New Deal and the philosophy of survival of the fittest, rugged individualism, and reactionary economics held by a majority of the Supreme Court. A fittingly grand setting was provided for the finale. The Court finally moved from the Capitol basement in 1932 into a home of its own, and a very fine one too.

From this citadel, during Roosevelt's first term, the conservative majority, occasionally joined by the liberal minority, turned down a string of measures designed to put the nation on the road to prosperity. Industrial recovery symbolized by the blue eagle was turned down in a famous "sick chicken" case. The Agricultural Adjustment Act met the same fate.

In other key decisions, Van Devanter, McReynolds, Sutherland, and Butler frequently had on their side Hughes, Chief Justice since Taft's death in 1930, and Sanford's successor, Owen J. Roberts, a Philadelphia lawyer who had made his national reputation as prosecutor of culprits in the Teapot Dome oil scandals of the 1920s.

Brandeis, eighty at the end of Roosevelt's first term and the oldest of the justices, was often joined by Harlan Fiske Stone, who had been Attorney General when Coolidge appointed him in 1925 and soon drifted out of the conservative camp, and Benjamin N. Cardozo, whose towering status as chief judge of New York's court of appeals virtually forced his appointment in 1932 when Holmes retired at ninety-one.

In Congress, and more virulently among labor leaders and reformers, "the nine old men" were denounced as antediluvian barriers to progress and recovery. Only Stone, Roberts, and Cardozo were under seventy, and Stone at sixty-one was the youngest.

The state of the economy improved during Roosevelt's first term, while fears of starvation and violent revolution faded. After the President's landslide election in 1936, victorious politicians were in no mood to see their cherished programs stifled by anachronistic judges.

This was an era of such profound change that some men called it "the Roosevelt revolution." It was also the time of the great split in the labor movement. In 1936 the AFL suspended and in 1937 expelled ten large unions that had formed a Committee (later Congress) of Industrial Organizations. More than domestic economic and social shocks were stirring the nation, including the bench, in the early months of 1937. Germany had launched a rearmament program after repudiating the World War I peace treaty. Civil War raged in Spain, where Germany and Italy were trying out new weapons. Congress was completing a series of neutrality acts—one each in 1935, 1936, and 1937—designed to avoid entanglement in threatening European conflicts by forbidding sale or shipment of arms to belligerents or giving them credit.

Into this setting fell the latest crisis in wages-and-hours legislation. While the nine old men listened to arguments in *West Coast Hotel Co. v. Parrish* et al. in December, six weeks after the election, the President was preparing what came to be known as his Court-packing bill. Its main feature was that if any Supreme Court justice did not resign six months after reaching the age of seventy, the President could add a new member to the Court. Passage would permit Roosevelt to name six new justices before the new year was half gone.

The case before the Court was clearly landmark material. Under a State of Washington statute for protection of women passed in 1913, Elsie Parrish, a chambermaid in the West Coast Hotel, was entitled to $14.50 for her forty-eight-hour week. She and her husband sued for the difference between this and the pay she actually received. (Neither those who argued the case nor those who decided it in the Supreme Court bothered to say how much this was.) The Parrishes lost in the trial court, which ruled the 1913 law unconstitutional, but won a judgment in the state supreme court. This time the hotel appealed, secure in the precedent of *Adkins*.

Between the time the justices heard arguments and March 29, 1937, when they announced their decision, the Court-packing debate had broken out and was the biggest news of the last weeks of winter.

With the irresistible electoral triumph so fresh in memory, the bill at first seemed unbeatable. Roosevelt made much of the popular feeling that doddering old men were unable to do their proper work of hearing legitimate cases and preferred to strike down progressive legislation just like farm hands abandoning their crops to shoot sparrows. But exactly one week before the *West Coast* ruling, Senator Burton K. Wheeler, leading the opposition in the upper house, read a letter from the Chief Justice dated the day before. Hughes, replying to a question Wheeler had asked, reported that the Court's docket was clear and had been for several years, a condition that has not prevailed for some time now. Hughes gave full details. His report, coupled with the Senator's indignation at the suggestion that Brandeis was too old to keep pace with the times—"unkind, to say the least"—doomed the bill.

The degree to which "the nine old men" were influenced by the Court-packing fight has been debated at great length, and support for almost any interpretation can be found. The fact is that Roosevelt lost in Congress but won in the Court. Van Devanter, McReynolds, Sutherland, and Butler clung to their rock-ribbed insistence that "the meaning of the Constitution does not change with the ebb and flow of economic events." But now they were in the minority.

Sutherland, who spoke for all four, repeated his *Adkins* opinion in essentials. Bitterly, he informed his colleagues that their power to interpret the Constitution is not the power to amend it, the usual cry of dissenters whose construction is rejected. Their opponents agree with them completely; they are sure they never make the law, never amend the Constitution, but merely expound it. Sutherland was not appeased by such disclaimers. He thought that changes in the rules "convert what was intended to be inescapable and enduring mandates into mere moral reflections."

The Chief Justice wrote the opinion of the Court, and after his long absence from the practice of law, Brandeis felt free to concur, which gave the overrulers their bare majority.

Hughes clearly relished the opportunity to turn his predecessor's dissent in *Adkins* into a Court about-face. He pointed out that the Constitution nowhere mentions freedom of contract, but only liberty. He added that "regulation which is reasonable in relation to the subject and is adopted in the interest of the community is due process." Referring to the Depression and the great burden placed on society by workers' inability to earn enough to support life, he declared:

"The community is not bound to provide what is in effect a subsidy for unconscionable employers. . . . Our conclusion is that the case of *Adkins v. Children's Hospital* should be, and it is, overruled."

The result was clearly due to Justice Roberts' change of mind. Not only had he voted more often against than for the New Deal, but only months before, he had joined the conservative quartet in ruling against New York's minimum wage law for women, which was very like that of Washington. The chief difference in the litigation was that the New York Court of Appeals had held the statute unconstitutional. Earlier in 1936, the Supreme Court verdict, as in *West Coast*, was 5 to 4 on *Morehead v. New York* ex rel. *Tipaldo*, and Roberts cast the deciding vote in each.

In form, the New York suit began as a habeas corpus action with Tipaldo, manager of a laundry, trying to get out of jail. He had been committed on an indictment charging that he refused to obey an order from state Industrial Commissioner Morehead to pay his women workers the prescribed minimum.

Butler wrote the opinion of the Court this time, affirming the decision of the court of appeals. Hughes dissented for himself, Stone, Brandeis, and Cardozo, with Stone adding a slightly stronger demand that *Adkins* be overruled here and now. Otherwise the reasoning on both sides followed very much the pattern of both *Adkins* and *West Coast*.

Roberts' swing vote marked the turn of the judicial tide toward due process decisions that conceded government's authority to deal realistically with new problems raised by increasing density of population, unprecedentedly complex combinations of business and labor, enormous industrial and technological expansion, and the emergence on earth of a nation of millions of people theoretically capable of supporting all of them at a high standard of living.

Under these conditions, and despite its Chief's longing for stability, order, and a fine respect for the opinions of his predecessors, the Hughes Court's five years quickened the pace of judicial about-faces.

9

A Day in Court for the Poor

The attitude toward the modern world that Justice Roberts exemplified soon had additional representation on the Court. Within a year after the *West Coast* decision, both Van Devanter and Sutherland retired. Senator Hugo Black of Alabama, whose thirty-four-year service was to be acclaimed as the most consistently "liberal" in history, became President Roosevelt's first appointee in 1937, succeeding Van Devanter.

Stanley F. Reed of Kentucky, who as Solicitor General had argued many New Deal cases, took Sutherland's seat. But the first about-face after the labor case occurred before Reed joined the

Court, and went back a great deal beyond the New Deal, to a ninety-six-year-old precedent that had been set by Justice Story.

For generations, Story had been revered among lawyers as a teacher, a commentator on the law, and an expounder of the Constitution. Nevertheless, his successors now pronounced his 1842 opinion not only mistaken but, for the only time in Supreme Court history, unconstitutional as well.

The paradoxical result was that the Hughes Court, busily establishing or justifying the most extensive Federal powers yet dreamed of, made a substantial concession to state authority, which the states' rights Taney Court had abrogated.

Both Courts were construing a clause in the Judiciary Act of 1789 that stated: "The laws of the several states, except where the Constitution, treaties, or statutes of the United States shall otherwise require or provide, shall be regarded as the rules of decision in the Courts of the United States, in cases where they apply." In other words, local rules should be followed in settling local disputes.

As has been seen in Chapters 2 and 4, the Supreme Court accepted this when real property was at stake. But in Story's time, commercial transactions were taking up more and more of the law's attention, and in 1842 his opinion in *Swift v. Tyson* made a distinction between land and the pieces of paper by which most business is conducted.

The problem was whether bills of exchange should be dealt with according to the rule established in the New York courts, which led to one interpretation, although the rule was different in other states. This indicated a lack of uniformity, and Story attempted to supply some national consistency to commercial law by allowing the Federal courts to exercise their own judgment as to what the local law should be when, as in this case, the dispute was between citizens of different states.

Story justified this authority to discriminate by saying that the decisions of any state's highest courts were not part of "the laws of the several States" but only what judges thought. So he deduced power for United States courts to create a national commercial code.

Here English precedents were useless. The United States, as the only large modern nation to adopt federalism, has spent nearly two hundred years trying to adjust the division of power suitably between state and national governments. This aspect of law is as ceaselessly subject to change as any other, when new developments dictate. Of course, experiments do not always work, which happened in 1842.

Instead of imposing uniformity, Story's ruling only increased the confusion. It added Federal versions to the contradictory rulings of the states, whose judges often ignored opinions from a United States court. Law was placed in the position of violating one of its own cardinal precepts—that it should be sufficiently precise that a man does not have to guess himself into jail or a lawsuit. Charles Warren, a leading historian of the Supreme Court, commented: "Probably no decision of the Court has ever given rise to more uncertainty as to legal rights . . . its chief effect has been to render it difficult for businessmen to know in advance to what particular topic the Court would apply the doctrine."

Warren wrote this before a denizen of Hugheston, Pennsylvania, Tompkins, walking along a path beside the Erie Railroad tracks on a dark night ninety-odd years after Story's opinion, was hit by an open door on a passing freight train. Tompkins sued the railroad, a New York corporation, in its home state so that he, as a citizen of another, could get his case into a Federal court.

His lawyers avoided Pennsylvania because courts there had held that a pedestrian walking parallel to the right of way rather than across it is a trespasser who must prove the railroad wilfully negligent before he can collect.

The Erie Railroad contended that Tompkins had been the negligent one, for he admitted he saw the train's headlights and heard it. He retorted that he had often been on this path when trains passed and never been hit before. Because the Pennsylvania rule was court-made and not contained in a statute, the United States district judge in New York applied his own idea of "general law" on the basis of Story's ruling, and let the case go to a jury, which awarded Tompkins thirty thousand dollars.

Only ten years earlier, the Supreme Court had upheld this procedure, and in a case where the victorious litigant had deliberately manipulated a "diversity of citizenship" to escape the operation of his own state's laws. The plaintiff was the Brown and Yellow Taxicab and Transfer Company of Bowling Green, Kentucky. In 1925 it had an exclusive franchise from the Louisville & Nashville Railroad to park cabs and solicit fares at the passenger station. The Black and White Taxicab and Transfer Company asserted a right to compete and, under the common law as construed by the Kentucky courts, could not be denied. So Brown and Yellow reincorporated in Tennessee and asked the United States court in Kentucky to enjoin Black and White from moving in on the station trade in taxis.

On the basis of *Swift v. Tyson* this was granted, and the Supreme Court agreed in a 1928 opinion by Butler, with Holmes and Brandeis dissenting.

Brandeis converted that dissent into the majority opinion in 1938, the only time he ever authored a Court about-face. The New York judge had erred in not following state rules that covered Tompkins' claim, he wrote.

Now in his last year on the bench, Brandeis was heeding a suggestion Holmes had made: "It is more important that this Court should be right upon later and more elaborate consideration of the cases than consistent with previous declarations."

In this field, however, the Court had previously adhered to a principle Brandeis himself put into words as ". . . in most matters it is more important that the applicable rule of law be settled than that it be settled right." Gracefully switching to the Holmes point of view, Brandeis credited Story with the best of motives, but pointed out that he had achieved the opposite of his intention.

As far back as 1892, Justice Field had protested the Story doctrine as allowing a judge to apply whatever rule he happened to favor. Holmes had denounced the practice as "an unconstitutional assumption of power by the courts of the United States which no lapse of time or respectable array of opinion should make us hesitate to correct."

Brandeis proceeded to correct it, saying that *Swift v. Tyson* had imposed an intolerable burden upon litigants and lawyers, that its "mischievous results had become apparent" and that it led to "injustice and confusion."

"The question for decision," he went on, "is whether the oft-challenged doctrine of *Swift v. Tyson* shall now be disapproved. . . . We hereby declare that in applying the doctrine this Court and the lower courts have invaded rights which in our opinion are reserved by the Constitution to the several states."

In that same term, the Court resumed its work of canceling favors that earlier decisions seemed to have extended to entrepreneurs at the expense of the public.

This particular about-face overturned a limitation on the taxing power that the Court, speaking through Holmes, had imposed in 1922 over the dissent of Pitney, Brandeis, and Clarke. The case had come up from Oklahoma and the majority found it reminiscent of one of Marshall's most famous cases, *McCullough v. Maryland,* by which states were forbidden to tax a Federal instrumentality, the Bank of the United States, on the much-quoted theory that the power to tax is the power to destroy.

One of Oklahoma's earliest actions as a state was to levy an income tax. It applied among other things to income derived from oil leases, and many of these leases were for land owned by Indians, so that the leases were negotiated with the Federal Government as guardian of the owners.

A man named Gillespie had leases on several tracts of Creek and Osage land, but he paid no tax on the income from 1915 through 1918. The state took him into a local court, whose judge ruled the tax unconstitutional because a Federal agency had done the leasing.

The state supreme court at first affirmed, but on a rehearing reversed, theorizing that the tax was on income, not on the lease. Gillespie found six justices of the Supreme Court who thought the state court had been right in the first place.

"A tax upon the leases," said Holmes, "is a tax upon the power to make them, and . . . a direct hamper upon the efforts of the United States to make the best terms that it can for its wards. . . . The same consideration that invalidates a tax upon the leases invalidates a tax upon the profits of the leases."

Sixteen years later the Court changed its mind by 5 to 2. Chief Justice Hughes for the majority—the dissenters, Butler and McReynolds, were the only two survivors of the 1922 majority—explained: "We are convinced that the rulings in *Gillespie v. Oklahoma* are out of harmony with correct principle and accordingly they should be, and they now are, overruled."

The extension of the *Gillespie* principle of tax immunity to any individual or corpation deriving income from public property was responsible for this about-face. The opportunity came about in this manner: The Mountain Producers Corporation filed a joint Federal tax return with a subsidiary taking oil from under Wyoming school lands, the state receiving a royalty of 65 percent. The corporation had claimed it did not have to pay income tax on its share, and for a dozen years had been winning in the lower courts on the ground that it was an agency of Wyoming so far as the operations on school lands were concerned.

The Collector of Internal Revenue finally brought the case before the Supreme Court. Hughes noted in his opinion that Wyoming held the land in trust for the schools, and he saw no interference with the execution of that trust, or with any other state function, if the oil company had to pay a tax on its income.

Even more representative of the Court's changes of mind in those years of accelerating technology and industrial growth while the world went into World War II was an about-face that the wages-and-hours decision had foreshadowed.

When the Government was held powerless to interfere with the liberty of men and women to contract for their labor, it certainly was not supposed to be able to usurp the family's prerogatives and prescribe rules of work for children. The Court had so held in 1918 by the narrow margin of 5 to 4 in invalidating a Congressional act of 1916 that barred from interstate commerce all products made by workers under fourteen and by those from fourteen to sixteen if they worked more than eight hours a day or six days a week or between the hours of 7 P.M. and 6 A.M.

Roland Degenhart of Charlotte, North Carolina, had sons who fell within each of these categories and were employed full time in a local cotton mill, which sold some of its wares outside North Carolina. As "next friend" and father of the boys, he asked the United States District Court to enjoin the United States Attorney from enforcing the 1916 law.

The judge obliged, and the Government appealed. Justice Day for himself, White, Van Devanter, Pitney, and McReynolds affirmed the decision. Child labor, they held, was governed exclusively by the police power of the states. Congress could presume to regulate only with regard to harmful products or activities—impure food and drugs, lottery tickets, and liquor. To attempt interference with anything as innocuous as child labor was doubly repugnant to the Constitution as transcending the authority given to Congress and asserting a power over purely local matters.

Holmes delivered a dissent in which McKenna, Brandeis, and Clarke joined. He thought no one would deny the right of

Congress to forbid certain goods from interstate commerce, and if
the prohibition had other effects that judges did not like, such as
ending mill work for young children, the law's validity was not
affected. Congress could choose its means for acting against
products it considered undesirable.

Holmes reminded his colleagues that Congress had so heavily
taxed oleomargarine colored to resemble butter that no one could
afford to make it except in its unappetizing white form (the dairy
lobby kept that one on the books for a long time) and surely
oleomargarine had been as much a matter for the states as cotton
cloth. Holmes waxed bitter over the majority's logic that a ban on
interstate transport "is permissible as against strong drink, but not
as against the product of ruined lives."

This minority view was not vindicated until after a Georgia
lumber manufacturer won a United States District Court order
quashing an indictment against him. He was accused of and did not
deny violating the Fair Labor Standards Act of 1938, which set
twenty-five cents an hour and extra pay for work over forty-four
hours a week in the production of goods destined for interstate
commerce.

The District Judge ruled that manufacturing was not interstate
commerce, so Congress could not interfere with conditions inside
a mill. He added that the intent of the legislation had not been to
regulate commerce between the states but to fix wages and hours
within them.

In 1918, the United States had been ending a world war; in
1941, it was entering one. In 1918, Congress passed a national
prohibition law while the Eighteenth Amendment was rushing to
ratification. By 1941, the prohibition era seemed as obsolete as
slavery. In 1918, no airplane had attained a speed of two hundred
miles an hour; by 1941, planes were flying routinely at twice that
speed. In 1918, war had pushed the total number of Federal civilian
employees over the half-million mark; in 1941, without yet getting
into war, the figure was a million.

Early in February 1941, the Supreme Court unanimously announced that the 1918 majority had departed from true constitutional principles, so their decision "should be and now is overruled." The justices were agreed now that Congress possessed full authority to regulate intrastate commerce whenever it affected interstate commerce. They added that the 1918 assertion that this power extended only to "deleterious" products was not only novel but had been unsupported.

By this time the Court had moved still further from the philosophy of the old diehards of due process, for whom McReynolds remained the only spokesman, and he was in his last year. Brandeis and Butler had been replaced by Felix Frankfurter, one further, one of Roosevelt's early advisers, and William O. Douglas, chairman of the New Deal's Securities and Exchange Commission.

A few weeks after the child labor case, they were both in the majority, with Douglas writing the opinion of the Court, to overturn another 1918 precedent. This reversal deprived other judges of a segment of their authority to punish critics for contempt.

The 1918 decision had been reached four years after the overheated municipal controversy that caused it. Fired by the example of Cleveland in instituting a three-cent streetcar fare, Toledo adopted an ordinance calling for a similar rate in that city after March 27, 1914.

The Toledo Railways and Light Company, which operated the streetcars and differed with the city fathers as to the expiration date of its franchise, resisted. It got the matter into the United States court by having some of its out-of-state creditors request an injunction to prevent the company from complying with the three-cent fare mandate.

The controversy over this motion raged for months, much of it outside the courtroom, especially in the columns of the Toledo *News Bee*. This daily, an ardent advocate of lower fares, made what Judge Killits, presiding in the local Federal court, considered not

only highly improper but outrageously unlawful comments meant
to influence his judgment. The character of the items to which he
took greatest exception was illustrated by a cartoon representing
the company as a dying man surrounded by sorrowing friends, one
of whom was saying: "Guess we'd better call in Doc Killits."

After the judge finally issued the injunction and drew another
blast from the *News Bee*, he declared the newspaper and its
managing editor guilty of contempt of court and fined them. The
circuit court of appeals affirmed, and the paper took its case to the
Supreme Court, partly on a plea of freedom of the press.

Chief Justice White, speaking for the Court, brushed aside this
First Amendment argument, saying that "to state it is to answer it,
since it involves in its very statement the contention that the
freedom of the press is the freedom to do wrong with impunity."
Attempts to intimidate judges must be punished, and the *News Bee*
remained fined.

Holmes and Brandeis dissented, a phrase that foreboded a fair
number of Supreme Court changes of mind. In this instance,
Holmes wrote for both, and he hinted that a judge who could be
intimidated by the sort of criticism shown in this record should
seek some other occupation. "I confess," Holmes said, "I cannot
find in this case anything that would have affected a mind of
reasonable fortitude, and still less can I find there anything that
obstructed the administration of justice."

Holmes's point was that the contempt power is given to judges
to protect their courts from interference and to punish offenses
committed in their presence, not to assuage their hurt feelings.
The district court faced no emergency justifying a contempt citation, Holmes thought, for Killits boasted while passing sentence
that he had endured the paper's abuse for six months.

What most people would consider a more reprehensible attempt
to tamper with a court than the *News Bee*'s crusade for the three-
cent fare set the stage for converting the Holmes-Brandeis dissent
into the opinion of a later Court.

In 1939, the son of an illiterate pauper named Elmore died after taking a patent medicine called BC, put out by a partnership, Council and Bernard, in Durham, North Carolina. Elmore sued the partners in the United States District Court, which, because he was "feeble in mind and body" as well as indigent, appointed a local lawyer, William B. Guthrie, to represent him. While the defendants were still preparing their answer to Elmore's complaint, R. H. Nye, whose daughter was married to Council's son, undertook to arrange matters. He had a tenant who lived near Elmore, some one hundred miles from Durham, and between them, through "use of liquor and persuasion," they got him to put his mark on papers asking that the suit be dismissed. Nye had his own lawyer draw up the documents, then took them to the post office and paid the registry fee and the postage.

When Guthrie brought these facts to the court's attention, the judge fined Nye $500 for contempt and the tenant $250, and also ordered Nye to pay Guthrie $500 for his services to Elmore.

When Nye's appeal reached the Supreme Court early in 1941, the justices all found his offense obnoxious, but six of them did not think a contempt citation was the appropriate remedy. Rather, they held, Nye should have been indicted and tried for conspiracy.

Douglas noted that the 1918 newspaper opinion had ignored rules for contempt procedures set up after Judge James H. Peck had been impeached in 1831 for imprisoning and disbarring a lawyer who criticized an opinion. Peck was acquitted, but James Buchanan, the future President, who managed the impeachment for the House, declared such a thing should never happen again, and the rules followed. They provided that an offense had to be committed in the presence or immediate neighborhood of the court to be liable for contempt, and the "evil influence" brought to bear on Elmore had been exerted one hundred miles away. The Court, therefore, had been wrong in the Toledo case, which was thereupon overruled. Hughes, Stone, and Roberts disagreed, preferring to leave broad contempt powers to the judges.

That year of 1941 was a great one for overrulings, at least seven by almost any criterion. One opened the way for the large migrations of poor people from the South to the North and West that have characterized the last thirty years. Another set the stage for a basic change in the rules governing party primaries.

The first of these two precedents was 104 years old, the most venerable yet to be reversed. It had been set in 1837 when the Court upheld a New York City ordinance requiring the master of a ship carrying passengers to list the age, place of birth, and occupation of each one landed. The law also allowed the city to demand a bond of up to $300 a head, posted by the captain, that the newcomers would not become public charges. The penalty for failure to comply was set at $75 per passenger.

On August 27, 1829, the ship *Emily*, just arrived from Liverpool, landed one hundred passengers in New York, and her captain, William Thompson, turned over no list. The city held the ship's consignee liable for the penalty and brought suit to collect it in superior court, but the defendant as an alien demanded that the case be transferred to Federal court.

Thereupon *The Mayor, Alderman, and Commonalty of the City of New York v. George Miln* began its somewhat protracted course of litigation. After several tries, the circuit court judges for the Southern District of New York could not agree on the constitutionality of the New York ordinance, and the Supreme Court first heard the case early in 1835 while Marshall was still alive. They did not decide it before he died, and it was reargued in the January term of 1837. All the justices except Story agreed that the city was merely exercising its police power to keep out undesirables and was not interfering with the regulation of interstate commerce, which was under the exclusive jurisdiction of Congress.

The opinion of the Court, written by one of the new members, Philip Barbour, said any state must have authority "to provide precautionary measures against the moral pestilence of paupers, vagabonds, and possibly convicts."

Story's dissent held that carrying passengers was a form of commerce and that anything affecting trade, even health regulations, must be left to Congress. He added that after the case was first argued, Marshall had expressed the opinion that the New York statute was unconstitutional.

American attitudes toward the poor had changed considerably in a century. The Great Depression had eradicated from many minds the belief that poverty had to be confined to the shiftless or the sinful. In 1837, it had been easy to believe that anyone could find at least subsistence in the vast domains of free land then to be had in a country with fewer than eight persons per square mile. By 1941, free land and the frontier were long gone, and the population was more than forty-four persons per square mile.

The majority rule of 1837 stood up until—during and after the Great Depression—very different patterns of migration began to prevail. For nearly one hundred years after *City v. Miln*, immigrants poured into United States ports by the millions every decade, reaching the peak of nearly nine million in the first ten years of the twentieth century. But the 1930s were the first decade since the 1830s that fewer than a million foreigners came to the United States to stay. Instead, the rush was from the country to the city and from South to North or West.

As had been the case with most European immigrants, poverty was the driving force. Before long relatively prosperous communities were crying out that the indigent and the helpless from other states were coming in droves to where relief payments were highest.

Under these circumstances, many people thought that laws to prevent an influx of the poor were perfectly reasonable, and California was one of the states that had erected such legal barriers. Anyone who, knowing a person was indigent, helped that person to enter California was guilty of a misdemeanor.

In December 1939, a resident of Marysville, California, named Edwards went to Spur, Texas, to bring back his wife's jobless brother, Frank Duncan, who had last worked for the Works Progress Administration, an early New Deal effort to combat unemployment. Edwards knew that Duncan had no more than twenty dollars when he left Spur, had spent most of it by the time he reached Marysville, and had no prospect of a job. He lived for ten days in the Edwards home and then "obtained financial assistance," as the court papers expressed it, from the Farm Security Administration.

Edwards, prosecuted for bringing an indigent into California, pleaded that the law was unconstitutional. His plea was denied, and he appealed a six-months suspended jail sentence.

Curiously enough, this case, like *City v. Miln*, was argued but not decided in the Chief Justice's last term. Hughes and McReynolds both retired after the spring term in 1941, Stone succeeding the Chief Justice. Senator James Byrnes of South Carolina and Robert H. Jackson, the Attorney General, were appointed during the summer and took their seats in time to hear *Edwards v. California* reargued in October. And as had been the case 104 years earlier, a new member, this time Byrnes, delivered the decision of the Court. He paraphrased with strong disapproval Barbour's 1837 pronouncement against the "moral pestilence of poverty" and declared:

"We do not consider ourselves bound by the language referred to. . . . Poverty and immorality are not synonymous."

Byrnes expressed some sympathy with the argument of California's Attorney General Earl Warren, appearing as a friend of the Court to defend the statute, that the Depression had added enormously to the problem of migrants. The justice conceded that a state might gain temporary respite by "shutting its gates to the outside world." But he quoted Cardozo, who once had opined that "in the long run prosperity and salvation are in union and not division."

"It is difficult to conceive of a statute," Byrnes commented, "more squarely in conflict with this theory than the Section [of the California law] challenged here."

Of course, Byrnes admitted, Cardozo's dictum was not part of the Constitution, and California was not bound by it. But the state was bound by the commerce clause, and transportation of people is commerce. Story had been correct in saying only Congress could regulate it. Byrnes took the trouble to add that the ruling would be the same if Duncan had been on local relief in both states. So if the poor were to be kept from moving across state lines, it would have to be a national, not a local, determination.

A hint that even Congress might not be able to do it was contained in concurring opinions by Douglas and Jackson, with which Black and Justice Frank Murphy, an earlier Roosevelt Attorney General elevated to the Court, agreed. They suggested that the Constitution protects people even more than goods or cattle. The immunities and privileges guaranteed to a citizen might preclude limitations on his access to any part of the country because of the state of his purse.

A 1941 decision that was a step toward another about-face, a quarter turn perhaps, came up from New Orleans. There, after the Democratic primary of 1940, the commissioners of elections had been indicted for changing eighty-three ballots cast for one congressional candidate and fourteen for another to a third in a Tenth Ward precinct. The United States District Court dismissed the charges on grounds that a party primary is a private matter that the United States election laws do not cover.

In one of the last decisions in which Hughes took part, the Supreme Court reversed the district judge, saying that indeed primaries are part of the election process, especially where, as in Louisiana, a primary victory is equivalent to election.

At the time, the Court did not mention a 1935 case, *Grovey v. Townsend*, a unanimous decision upon which the New Orleans judge had relied. Grovey, a black man, had asked Clerk Townsend of Harris County, Texas, for a Democratic primary ballot and had been turned down on the ground that a 1932 resolution of the State Democratic Convention restricted party membership to whites.

Grovey sued in justice court for damages of ten dollars and lost. Texas law gave him no right to seek appeal further in the state, so he went directly to the Supreme Court. That body informed him that while it had outlawed state regulations barring Negroes from primaries, the Democratic Convention's rule was not state action, and so he had no legal redress. The opinion was unanimous.

It was still the law of the land seven years later when Smith, another black man in Harris County, tried to vote in the 1942 primary to choose candidates for United States Senator and Representative. Since this was a contest for national office, he sought his rights in the Federal court, and his opinion of the value of a vote was higher than Grovey's. He asked $5,000 from the election judges who had refused to give him a ballot. Losing in this attempt and in the circuit court of appeals, he persisted to the Supreme Court, where his case was argued in November 1943.

By this time, a good many people were retreating from the lily-white prejudices. A few Jim Crow barriers had fallen, a few Judge Lynch rulings had been condemned. In the midst of a war in which black men were fighting beside whites to defeat, among other things, the racial policies of Nazi Germany, denial of the right to vote solely on grounds of color became increasingly absurd. Furthermore, since 1935 Federal participation in almost every aspect of national life had broadened to unprecedented dimensions.

In this case of *Smith v. Allwright*—the defendant was the Harris County election judge—it helped that Justice Roberts was the only member of the 1935 Court still sitting. He was the only one who stood by the *Grovey* decision. The others cited the New Orleans opinion to show that a Federal interest in primaries exists. They also pointed out that primaries are held according to laws promulgated by the states and are conducted under the authority of the states. That, the opinion said, brings these elections under the Fifteenth Amendment, which forbids abridgment by the states of any citizen's right to vote on account of race or color.

In view of this rather obvious fact, the majority proceeded to overrule *Grovey v. Townsend* by name, adding that "When convinced of former error this Court has never felt constrained to follow precedent."

At this stage in a review of how the Court changes its mind, the statement seems a little obvious, although perhaps "hardly ever" would have been more accurate. Sometimes, after all, the majority has felt as Justice Roberts did in this case:

"The reason for my concern is that the instant decision, overruling that announced about nine years ago, tends to bring the adjudications of this tribunal into the same class as a restricted railroad ticket, good for this day and train only."

❧ **10** ❧

New Light on Old Freedoms

The "good for this day and train only" gibe would have been much more appropriate a year earlier when Justice Roberts was in the minority, objecting to an about-face in connection with one of the most persistent modern invokers of constitutional rights, the Jehovah's Witnesses. Their stubborn adherence to their special brand of Christianity has rubbed established society the wrong way so often that their lawyer, Hayden C. Covington, is said to have argued more often in the Supreme Court than anyone, except possibly Thurgood Marshall, when he was counsel for the National Association for the Advancement of Colored People, and

John W. Davis, whose services were sought by clients at the highest level for half a century.

Great advocacy, of which such men are capable, performs the important function of inspiring change—sometimes. Acute reasoning goes further in this direction than eloquence.

Counsel for the Witnesses have plenty of opportunity to exercise this talent, for the sect has never accepted secular rulings that contradict its religious beliefs in any particular, not even those handed down by the august bench in Washington. So no one was surprised when in March 1943 the Witnesses were back to appeal two quite different rulings that had been handed down against them on the basis of Supreme Court opinions delivered as little as one and three years earlier. This time, one can hardly attribute the overruling to changing conditions, even though, as in the first about-face of all in 1810, the world was at war.

The cases that had gone against the Witnesses were *Minersville School District v. Gobitis*, 1940, and *Jones v. Opelika*, 1942. The Court's about-face on both seems due to second thoughts among some of the justices, since seven of the nine who rendered judgment in 1940 were still on the bench in 1943. McKenna left shortly after *Gobitis*, and President Roosevelt nominated his Attorney General, Robert H. Jackson. Chief Justice Hughes also retired after the 1940 decision and before *Jones v. Opelika*. Justice Byrnes, who was named to complete the Court when Stone became Chief Justice, heard the 1942 case, but resigned—the first justice to serve only a year since 1793—to be replaced by Wiley B. Rutledge in time for the overruling case.

The 1940 lawsuits attracted more attention. Lillian and William Gobitis, aged twelve and ten, had been expelled from the public school in Minersville, Pennsylvania, because they refused to salute the United States flag, as commanded by an official regulation. Their religion forbade such idolatry, as the Jehovah's Witnesses interpreted the act. The lower court held that members of even a small, unpopular sect are entitled to the free exercise of their religion, and if that ruled out salutes to national symbols, the community would have to accept it.

The school district appealed, and in 1940 Justice Felix Frankfurter wrote for a majority of eight that this was not a field in which judges have special competence. Rather, he said, they should leave such matters to be fought out in the forum of public opinion, which would then be reflected by appropriate legislation interpreted by the state courts. Therefore, flag salutes were indisputably within the exclusive province of the states. Any interference with education officials on this score would make the Supreme Court the nation's school board, Frankfurter feared.

The opinion indicated that, like the rest of the country, the Court's majority was concerned with the threat posed to the United States by the war, which was still confined to the European powers. "National unity is the basis of national security," Frankfurter wrote, so that if a state considered the salute to be a step toward such unity, it was not for Federal judges to interpose any obstacle. Frankfurter recalled a warning Lincoln once uttered against becoming too weak to maintain our liberties. Therefore, the injunction against the school board should be withdrawn and the Gobitis children left to the mercies of Pennsylvania law. Stone, not yet Chief Justice, registered the lone dissent.

On the strength of this ruling, West Virginia in 1941 amended its education statutes to provide that children in public schools salute the flag in "the commonly accepted form" of placing the right hand on the breast while reciting the Pledge of Allegiance. Children failing to perform this rite could be expelled. They then became liable to prosecution as delinquents—being unlawfully absent from school—and their parents to a fine of fifty dollars and thirty days in jail.

Jehovah's Witnesses protested that this forced their children to violate their religious beliefs. They offered to have pupils of their faith recite an expression of respect for the flag and of obedience to all laws consistent with God's law. The State of West Virginia rejected this compromise, and the Witnesses went to the United States District Court for an injunction to prevent the Board of Education from enforcing the statute against their children. The evidence showed that students had been threatened with the reformatory if they failed to salute. The district court ignored the *Gobitis* decision and granted the injunction. The Board of Education appealed.

Meanwhile in the states of Alabama, Arkansas, and Arizona, Jehovah's Witnesses were in trouble with the law on another count. One of their forms of evangelism is the distribution of tracts on streets or by knocking on doors. They solicit money, five cents to a quarter usually, but often leave the leaflets whether paid for or not. They therefore ran afoul of ordinances that require street and house-to-house vendors to obtain a license, for which a small fee is exacted. This, too, is against the word of God, as the Witnesses hear it, and so in 1942 the Supreme Court was called upon to rule on their claim of Witness Jones to be exempted from the vendor's license law of Opelika, Alabama. The majority again found no genuine interference either with freedom of religion or of speech. When a religious group uses the streets to sell their propaganda, the state can reasonably exact the same fee it requires others to pay under the same circumstances. That might seem to be the end of that, but in view of still more cases coming up on the same subject, the Court agreed to another hearing.

The Supreme Court has the faculty of keeping its sense of proportion when even so great an emergency as all-out war is causing other agencies and branches of the government, including lesser courts, to lose theirs. A constitutional issue is no more and no less urgent in times of turmoil than in times of tranquillity. Thus, in 1942, the Court set a basic rule in the development of civil aviation when it found against the Government in favor of Thomas and Tinie Causby, whose chicken farm was being ruined by bombers taking off and landing at an adjoining airport. The amount of money at stake was two thousand dollars.

The reargument of *Jones v. Opelika*, the first argument in a similar case, *Murdoch v. Pennsylvania*, and the West Virginia Board of Education's appeal were all heard on March 10 and 11, 1943. The peddling decision was the first delivered, on May 3, and the Court, through Justice Douglas, chose for its detailed opinion to consider the conviction of Murdoch, a Jehovah's Witness, for violating a forty-year-old ordinance of Jeanette, Pennsylvania, requiring street vendors to take out licenses.

Douglas and four colleagues thought it was possible to draw a line between commercial peddling and the age-old form of missionary evangelism in which the Witnesses engage. Douglas called it a distortion of the facts to label the sect as engaged in the occupation of selling. The freedoms mentioned in the First Amendment, he added, are not guaranteed only to those who can pay for the privilege, and as for the precedent set the year before:

"The judgment in *Jones v. Opelika* has this day been vacated. Freed from the controlling precedent, we can restore to their high constitutional position the liberties of itinerant evangelists."

Justice Reed for the four minority members dissented on the ground that the case involved itinerant merchants. A sale is a sale, he said, and while making their house-to-house canvasses the Witnesses are clearly engaged in the occupation of selling. The Constitution never meant to prevent the type of regulation involved here, he maintained.

Justice Frankfurter, concurring in this, added a long dissent of his own in which he pointed out that even the Witnesses did not say the license requirement would be financially burdensome or impair their ability to exercise their constitutional rights. They claimed immunity from any tax on the distribution of religious literature. But, Frankfurter argued, that tax applies to all, not merely to the religious. He found it as thoroughly justified as the income tax on a clergyman's salary or a requirement that everyone abide by health regulations even if these run counter to religious beliefs. As to a suggestion by the majority that an entering wedge of tax can be dangerous, he quoted Holmes who once had said: "The power to tax is not the power to destroy as long as this Court sits."

Six weeks later, on June 14, the opinions on saluting the flag were read. In the previous three years, during which we had entered the war and were rebounding from initial disasters, patriotism had risen to an uncommon pitch. Yet the regimentation implied in the legislated homage to a national emblem had gained little ground in the hearts of Americans. We were supposed to be fighting against a system personified by Nazi and Fascist parades and pomp punctuated by shouts and well-drilled gestures. The compulsory salute in American schools—most used the "stiff arm" variety rather than the hand on breast, no matter what the law said—smacked a little too much of our enemies to be universally palatable. At the same time, a revulsion of popular feeling against the abuse heaped upon the Jehovah's Witnesses after the *Gobitis* decision had taken place among many who were inclined to respect a religious stand even if they did not agree with it.

Whether this was a consideration among the justices or not, Black, Douglas, and Murphy announced that they had changed their minds since 1940. They explained that they had then been reluctant to interfere with state regulation of citizens' conduct. They still thought the principle sound, but reflection and *Jones v. Opelika* had convinced them that it did not apply in this case. Murphy added a strong expression of distaste for what he now saw as an attempt at compulsion in matters of conscience.

These remarks came in concurring opinions. Justice Jackson spoke for the Court's majority of six to overrule *Gobitis*. He took great care to answer the main points of that decision. He deferred to Lincoln, but he doubted that the Great Emancipator would have thought the strength of government impressively vindicated by expelling a few children from school. Far from becoming a school board itself, the Court protects people from government officials of all kinds, including school officials, who, because they educate children for citizenship, should be held to very strict constitutional accountability. Jackson did not like Frankfurter's idea of leaving this field to the forum of public opinion. The Bill of Rights was adopted, he pointed out, to remove certain subjects from the political arena, and religion is one. Judges need no special competence in either religion or education to spot invasions of legal rights. Finally, Jackson remarked, unity is a fine goal, but the Constitution gives no one the power to compel it, and the experience of man from the Roman drive against Christianity to "the fast-failing efforts of our present totalitarian enemies" is that moderate measures lead to harsher ones so that: "Compulsory unification of opinion achieves only the unanimity of the graveyard."

Jackson wrote more than a rebuttal to *Gobitis*, however. He found no attempt in this school legislation to teach anything, to tell children what the flag stands for. To him, the question was not whether nonconformist beliefs should be exempted from a ceremony, but whether the state had any power to prescribe the salute and Pledge of Allegiance as a legal duty for anyone, which the *Gobitis* ruling had assumed.

"The sole conflict," Jackson declared, "is between authority and the right of the individual. If there is any fixed star in our constitutional constellation, it is that no official, high or petty, can prescribe what shall be orthodox in politics, nationalism, religion, or other matters of opinion, or force citizens to confess by word or act their faith therein."

Roberts, Reed, and Frankfurter held to their views of three years before, with Frankfurter adding a long separate dissent on why he believed the salute should be left to legislation. He thought the majority were trying to imply that if legislation is constitutional it must be wise, and vice versa. But for him the interests of civilization must be realized outside the courts. While he clearly did not like compulsory salutes any better than Jackson did, he conceded to the people the right to err.

These two overrulings became themselves precedents for later denials of governmental power to require loyalty oaths or curb the conscience of citizens. Handed down in the midst of war, which usually demands far more conformity than peace, the decisions were remarkable for the fact that the Court could reach them and for the quite general public acquiescence. They were unusual, too, in that they happened only because several justices changed their minds on the same issue at the same time, and frankly said so.

The Court during and soon after the war made several other about-faces. As the spur of an all-out martial effort accelerated the pace of change, the justices returned to the general pattern set by their predecessors—discovery that a precedent, not necessarily venerable but usually reaffirmed many times, has become out-moded. A good example was the judicial view of the insurance business. In 1869 a unanimous Court had set forth a number of interesting findings in affirming a fine of fifty dollars imposed on Samuel Paul of Petersburg, Virginia, for selling a fire insurance policy written by a New York company.

Virginia had a law that no insurance company not incorporated in the state could do business there without a license and posting a bond of from $30,000 to $50,000—an enormous sum at that time. Neither of these conditions was required of local insurance companies. Paul applied for a license as a representative of several New York underwriters, offering to comply with all regulations except posting the bonds. Denied a license, he sold a policy anyway to test the law, and the case came to the Supreme Court on appeal from a ruling by the supreme court of appeals in Virginia that Paul's conviction was valid.

Lawyers for Paul attacked the constitutionality of the statute on two grounds. First, it violated the provision that "the citizens of each state shall be entitled to all the privileges and immunities of citizens in the several states." Second, it infringed the commerce clause, because only Congress could regulate interstate commerce. Two short passages from the opinion, written by Justice Field, disposed of these arguments and the case.

As to the first contention, it was "a fact that corporations are not citizens." As to the second: "Issuing a policy of insurance is not a transaction of commerce."

Field explained that it is merely a contract, and not even in effect until it is in the insured's hands, so it is a purely local matter even if it could be called commerce.

Seventy-five years later, a group of insurance companies tried to apply that second point to their own benefit. The South-Eastern Underwriters Association, accused by the Government of anti-trust law violations, invoked Justice Field's definition, since the Sherman Act applied only in interstate commerce. The Field rule had been consistently followed all this time, too. In 1944 the Court was closely divided on the issue, with neither Roberts nor Reed taking part. The majority said insurance was indeed commerce. The minority, led by Chief Justice Stone, did not dispute the factual finding, but they would not on their own repudiate "this long continued and consistent construction of the commerce clause." Their point was that Congress had had ample time to bring insurance under the Sherman Act if it wanted to, but it had never done so.

This about-face was highly unusual because only four justices voted for it. The Court has rarely overruled a prior decision with less than a majority of the total of all judges. The minority, furthermore, was on ground that the Court usually takes when Congress has a chance to correct the outmoded precedent without a constitutional amendment. Stone paraphrased Brandeis, saying ". . . the rule of *stare decisis* embodies a wise policy because it is often more important that a rule of law be settled than that it be settled right. . . . it is the duty of the Court to make certain that more harm will not be done in rejecting than in retaining a rule of even dubious validity."

However, when Congress does make a correction, the Supreme Court may be called upon to pick up the pieces for years after-wards. In the process, it has been known to overrule the decision that inspired the Congressional action. A case entitled *May v.*

Heiner set off such a series of events, not the least interesting of which was a demonstration of how quickly Congress can respond to a certain type of stimulus. At one point, the unanimous ruling of the Court on one day was overturned the very next day by a Joint Resolution introduced into the legislative mill only at that moment.

It started in 1917 in what must have seemed a clever way to avoid the new Federal inheritance tax enacted the year before, the first since the Civil War. On October 1, Pauline May of Pennsylvania set up a trust fund of bonds, notes, and corporate stocks for her four children. However, all the income was to go to her husband Barney during his lifetime and to her for her lifetime if she survived him. That is what happened, and when she died in 1920, Collector of Internal Revenue Heiner tried to collect an estate tax on the amount of the trust fund. The heirs retorted that they had not inherited the fund in 1920; their mother had given it to them in 1917 and so no tax was due. (The Federal gift tax was instituted only in 1924.) The Collector insisted. The estate finally paid but sued in the district court in Media, Pennsylvania, for a refund.

The judge held in effect that the trust was a device to evade taxes, because in fact the May children only got the property as a result of their mother's death. The court of appeals agreed.

The pace of estate litigation is notoriously slow, so the Supreme Court did not hear arguments in this case until March 7, 1930. On April 14, a unanimous bench, speaking through Justice McReynolds, held that the Mays had hit upon a perfectly legal detour around the tax because the heirs were in legal possession of the trust before their mother died even if they got no income from it.

"The transfer of October 1st, 1917, was not made in contemplation of death, within the legal significance of those words," the Court decided. "It was not testamentary in character and was beyond recall by the decedent."

Although 1917 was the first year the Federal Government took in more than a billion dollars ($101,000,000 more), taxes were collected at the rate of less than eight dollars per capita. Twenty years later, the rate was nearly three hundred dollars. The national debt, below a billion dollars when the United States entered World War I in 1917, was 280 billion after World War II. Of course, the Federal Government was in debt when it was formed in 1789 (inheriting the Revolutionary War obligations) and never has been free of it, although it came very close in 1835 when the national debt stood at $35,513.

It took a year for the Treasury Department to grasp the full import of the *May* ruling. Then, on March 2, 1931, the Supreme Court granted the appeals of three more estates seeking refunds on the strength of *May v. Heiner.* On March 3, Acting Secretary of the Treasury Ogden Mills wrote to the Speaker of the House that if this continued, the Government would lose a third of its estate tax revenue and have to refund $25 million or more besides. As Senator Reed Smoot, chairman of the Senate Finance Committee, reported in urging legislative haste, the news "came almost like a bombshell." Before night, both Houses had passed and the President had signed a resolution closing the loophole the Mays had opened in the tax laws.

The resolution, however, was not retroactive. Before March 4, 1931, a good many trusts had been created, and from time to time the Collectors of Internal Revenue brought the heirs to court when they claimed exemption from estate taxes. The Treasury was frustrated, envying its state counterparts who collected under their own laws because their courts, ignoring *May v. Heiner,* held that the trust device was a fiction to evade, not avoid taxes. Finally, in 1940, the Supreme Court did allow the Collector his bite out of a trust that had gone to the children of Anne Lamson Hallock. The trust had been created by her husband as part of a separation agreement in 1919. She was to receive the income for her life. If she died before him, the property was to revert to him; if not, the children were to receive it on her death. Actually, Mr. Hallock died first, but the Supreme Court held that the possibility of reversion to him removed the trust from the sanctuary of *May v. Heiner*. Justice Frankfurter, who inclined more than most of his colleagues to accept *stare decisis*, which the lawyers for the Hallocks pleaded, delivered the Court's opinion. He made a neat distinction between reason and *stare decisis*, saying that neither bound the Court to persist in error, but he did not actually overrule *May v. Heiner*.

That was in 1944 after a long struggle. In 1924, Francois L. Church of New York City, then twenty-one years old, put one thousand shares of stock in the family business, the Church & Dwight Company of Maine, into a trust of which he and his brothers, Charles and Dwight, were trustees. The income was to be paid to Francois for life, then to his children if he had any, and if not, to his surviving brothers and sisters. He died childless in 1939. His executors successfully pleaded *May v. Heiner* in both the court of tax appeals and the Court of Appeals for the Second Circuit. The Commissioner of Internal Revenue persisted, so the Supreme Court heard arguments in October 1947, rearguments in October 1948, and reached a decision in January 1949.

By this time, two changes had been made on the bench. Stone died in 1946 and was succeeded as Chief Justice by Fred M. Vinson of Kentucky, who, like Salmon P. Chase, was Secretary of the Treasury when appointed. Justice Roberts retired in 1945, to be replaced by Harold H. Burton of Ohio. This time a majority of six was ready to find *May v. Heiner* mistaken, and overruled it frankly. Black, writing for the Court, recited the history of the trust device in some detail. The issue hinged, in his view, on the meaning of the words "possession and enjoyment" in the tax laws. By "century-old historic meaning and the long-standing Treasury interpretation," he said, title to property requires both, but in this case only Francois Church had any enjoyment of the trust during his lifetime. Therefore, it could hardly be said that his brothers had any title to it, for, until he died, their possession was empty. While *Hallock* had not specifically overruled the 1930 decision, he added, it "unequivocally rejected the only support that could possibly suffice for the holdings in *May v. Heiner*" because *Hallock* said the trusts did have a testamentary character. Black indicated that his dislike of the tactic may have influenced his opinion, for he commented on the results of the Mays's enterprise:

"Preparation of papers to defeat an estate tax thus became an easy chore for one skilled in the various niceties of the art of conveyance."

Finally, he dismissed a plea that the Churches were entitled to rely on "stability" in the law, meaning the 1930 precedent. Black pointed out that when Francois Church executed his trust, Treasury regulations subjecting such accumulations of property to an estate tax when the creator died were in effect and would not be overturned until six years later. Before that, the lower court rulings had gone against the estate, so Church could hardly have been relying on any judicial precedent.

Reed, Frankfurter, and Burton dissented in separate opinions. Frankfurter's is the most interesting because he reconciled his *Hallock* opinion with his acceptance of *May*. He noted that in the 1931 affirmations of that ruling, the revered Hughes, Holmes, Brandeis, and Stone were all in accord with that interpretation of the law. Furthermore, the Congressional resolution was not retroactive. Frankfurter repeated that the Hallock trust was not like the May trust since Hallock kept a reversionary interest for himself, not merely the income. The distinction was enough, the Justice thought, that the *May* rule was not binding then as he considered it to be now.

The net result of this decision was that trusts such as those Mrs. May and Hallock set up before 1931 were taxed as inheritance from then on. The majority's reasoning in *Church*, if it had prevailed in 1930 when the Treasury argued for it, would have sustained the Collector's ruling and rendered the Joint Resolution of Congress unnecessary.

One other about-face executed by the Vinson Court started the country along the road that has led from strict censorship of motion pictures on what were termed moral grounds to today's climate of "anything goes." The decision reflected, if faintly, the immense changes in popular notions of what is fit to be seen and heard publicly in this country between pre-World War I and post-World War II. People at either end would be horrified by the views and attitudes held by those at the other. The law that satisfied the nation in 1915 would be impossible to enforce today even if it had been allowed to remain on the books, like remnants of old blue laws that have never been repealed but would be if anyone tried to enforce them. During these decades, censorship of films has traveled perhaps the most clearly marked legal road of any art or medium of communication.

One of the first milestones along that road was set up in a number of states in the form of boards of review or commissions of censors to which all movies intended for public exhibition had to be submitted. No picture that failed to obtain the censor's approval could be shown legally. The Ohio version, which came to be the one tested in the Supreme Court, was typical. Adopted in 1913, it created a board within the State Industrial Commission to license all films exhibited to the public. The board was instructed to pass only those that it found "moral or educational, amusing and harmless." The Mutual Film Corporation, a major distributor, protested that it would be impossible to submit all its 2,500 reels or more to the censors or for that body to review them fast enough to prevent the business from being ruined. Their appeal from an adverse state ruling reached the Supreme Court early in 1915, along with a similar one from Kansas, and the Court chose to base its detailed opinion on the Ohio case.

Justice McKenna delivered that opinion, and he had hardly started before it was clear that the art of film had not impressed the bench as particularly important in American life. When he finished, no dissenters took occasion to prophesy that the movies might yet play a role in influencing people that would merit some consideration of censorship's implications. The corporation had based its case on three propositions, and McKenna knocked them down in rapid succession.

First, Mutual Film asserted, a compulsory review and license of all motion pictures shown in a state was an unreasonable burden upon interstate commerce, which states are forbidden to impose. Virtually every reel shown was manufactured outside of Ohio, and by the time the board got around to all of them, many would be valueless. McKenna replied that the films were not censored on coming into the state, only after they were already there, and so "we can immediately put to one side the contention that it imposes a burden on interstate commerce."

Second, said the corporation, the First Amendment guarantee of free speech forbids pre-censorship. Otherwise, the medium is in the same position as the press in England had been when every publication had to be licensed by the Crown. Not so, said McKenna, because ". . . the exhibition of moving pictures is a business pure and simple, originated and conducted for profit, like other spectacles, not to be regarded, nor intended to be regarded by the Ohio Constitution, we think, as part of the press of the country or organs of public opinion." Writing, speaking, and printing are the activities that the First Amendment protects, according to McKenna. He put the movies in the same category as the theater or a circus, which the state was empowered to regulate. The opinion did not mention, however, that no state required pre-censorship or licensing of a stage play or vaudeville performance.

Third, the appeal urged, the Ohio statute was drawn in such broad terms that it constituted an improper delegation of legislative powers to the board of censors. The legislators had set up no guidelines as to what was "moral," "educational," "amusing," or "harmless." McKenna met this by declaring that the legislature was well within its powers in relying upon "the sense and experience of men" to establish standards that would carry out the law's intent.

As an aside perhaps, rather than an answer to any points raised in the arguments, McKenna announced that no evidence had been presented that any good film ever had been rejected by the censors. The Ohio statute was valid on all counts.

On these grounds, pre-censorship of the movies soon became a widespread state activity. It has been said that no man ever was wise enough to be a censor and few wise enough to refuse to try. The men and women who put the seal of approval or disapproval on movies were no exceptions. But the world and the medium changed in spite of the censors, although for more than thirty-five years they had *Mutual Film Corporation v. Industrial Commission of Ohio* to fall back on when their commands were questioned. Eventually they found that the Supreme Court had moved with the times somewhat faster and farther than they had.

Censorship of the communications media and arts was an old story. It had reached its most puritanical pitch before movies were popular, but the screen continued to be rigorously inspected and expurgated even after the bars began to drop for stage and print. The scourge of the arts, Anthony Comstock, had his first reverse in 1905 when he tried to close *Mrs. Warren's Profession*, written by a man Comstock called "this Irish smut peddler," better known as George Bernard Shaw. A three-man court acquitted the play's producer by a vote of 2 to 1, although the drama dared mention prostitution. Books began their liberation in 1913 when Judge Learned Hand dismissed a Comstock raid on Mitchell Kennerley, publisher of *Hagar Revelly* by Daniel Carson Goodman, which also dealt with prostitution. The screen was held to far stricter rules and had far fewer defenders.

The film that led the Supreme Court to overrule itself on movie pre-censorship actually had been duly and properly licensed by New York's censors, and was shown for ten days before it got into trouble with the law. *The Miracle*, directed by Roberto Rossellini, starring Anna Magnani, backed by critical acclaim after its premiere at the 1948 Venice film festival, opened in this country on December 12, 1950, using English subtitles. It had the blessing of the motion picture division of the New York Education Department, the official licensing agency. Because it ran only forty minutes, it was made part of a trilogy with two French movies under the title *Ways of Love*, at a theater specializing in foreign films.

The Miracle tells of a girl who, while tending her goats, mistakes a bearded stranger for Saint Joseph and begs him to take her to heaven. Falling asleep after their conversation and the wine he provides, she is not sure on waking that the episode was not a dream. A priest tells her that it is possible she really did see a saint. Her pregnancy, revealed later, subjects her to such cruel mockery from old and young alike that she takes refuge in a lonely cave. When her time comes, she stumbles out seeking help, but manages only to reach an empty church, where she bears her child. The film closes with a baby crying in the background while an exalted girl exclaims, "My son! My love! My life!"

To many New York Catholics, the story seemed blasphemous, and blasphemy rather than obscenity has drawn the Church's thunder. The official *Index Expurgatorius*, begun in 1555, never listed a book for its sexual content. In this case, in Italy, the Vatican's Catholic Cinematographic Center had denounced the film, but the Vatican had not requested the Italian Government to suppress *The Miracle*, as it was entitled to do under the concordat that governed Papal-Italian relations. Some New Yorkers, however, are inclined to be "more Catholic than the Pope," and two days before Christmas 1950, City License Commissioner Edward T. McCaffrey informed the theater he would cancel its license if it continued to show the film. A state judge told the Commissioner that his position did not make him an arbiter of morals, taste, or propriety, and enjoined him from interfering. *The Miracle* returned to the screen. It won the New York Film Critics'

Award as the best foreign picture of the year and an endorsement from the National Board of Review, a private group not connected with the industry, as "especially worth seeing."

On January 7, 1951, Cardinal Spellman entered the controversy by ordering a call for stricter censorship read at mass in Saint Patrick's Cathedral. Although many other Catholics found *The Miracle* inoffensive, and said so publicly, hundreds of complaints poured in upon the State Board of Regents, statutory supervisor of the Education Department. Its chancellor asked three members to review the film, and on the basis of their report held a hearing February 10 at which Commissioner of Education Wilson was ordered to rescind the license. The movie's importer, Joseph Burstyn, appealed, but lost in the New York courts, so on April 24, 1952, *Joseph Burstyn Inc. v. Wilson* was argued before the Supreme Court.

In all cases, but especially in those involving fundamental constitutional rights, advocacy may and sometimes does play an important role in the decision. Justices do have open minds—not all of them on the same subjects, perhaps, so that facts and principles voiced by genuinely talented counsel can influence the bench. Censorship is a subject that has inspired more than common eloquence, not only among the bar but in judges. In this instance, the oral arguments and the briefs, including one submitted by the American Civil Liberties Union, a frequent "friend of the court" in these matters, were especially keen and forceful. No one can ever know, of course, the extent to which that day's advocacy affected the justices, but the result was three separate opinions saying that the attempted suppression of *The Miracle* was unconstitutional and also that movies must be freed from the pre-censorship permitted by the *Mutual Film* case thirty-seven years before. Justice Clark wrote the unanimous opinion of the Court; Reed delivered one concurrence for himself alone and Frankfurter another in which Jackson and Burton joined.

Counsel had covered many points, Clark noted, but he kept his opinion to the issue of free speech, for that was enough on which to reverse the New York courts' judgment against Burstyn. This, the justice went on, was the first case since *Mutual Film* to pose the question whether movies "are within the ambit of protection which the First Amendment, through the Fourteenth, secures to any form of 'speech' or 'the press.' " Then: "It cannot be doubted that motion pictures are a significant medium for the communication of ideas . . . not lessened by the fact that they are designed to entertain as well as to inform."

That they are a business organized for profit is irrelevant, Clark pointed out, for so is most of the press. The Constitution, therefore, protects *The Miracle* in picture form just as it would if the story were told in print. He cited a number of decisions against prior restraint of newspapers, magazines, books, and pamphlets. So: "To the extent that language in the opinion of *Mutual Film Corporation v. Industrial Commission of Ohio* . . . is not in harmony with the views here set forth, we no longer share it."

Clark made it clear that the Court did not mean all pictures could be shown at all times in all places. What the Court struck down was denial in advance of permission to communicate ideas. The New York courts had said no one should be allowed to ridicule religion. The Supreme Court replied, ". . . the state has no legitimate interest in protecting any or all religions from views distasteful to them."

Justice Reed expressed succinctly his agreement that the First Amendment is binding on the states and that *The Miracle* is not the kind of material it permits states to suppress. He implied that other ideas might not be so protected.

Justice Frankfurter's concurring opinion went beyond First Amendment considerations to declare that the ruling against the picture as "sacrilegious" was invalid because the word is too vague in meaning to let people know what is forbidden—as bad as the words in the Ohio statute of 1913 now condemned. "Sacrilegious" gains no precision "from the sense and experience of men," on which Justice McKenna relied in his 1915 opinion, Frankfurter said. In an appendix, he printed seven and a half pages of definitions from thirty-four authorities between 1651 and 1875. Historically, he recalled, "sacrilege" in English law was confined to stealing from a church or damaging church property—but only of the Established Church. The statute had been repealed less than a century ago. Nevertheless, Frankfurter was not condemning every suppression of movies at all times, any more than Clark did. Frankfurter explained that certainly freedom of speech would not extend to a showing of *The Miracle* in windows facing Saint Patrick's Cathedral on Easter Sunday morning. He summed up his view of the basis for all such opinions as the Court was now delivering: "The Constitution, we cannot recall too often, is an organism, not merely a literary production."

It is as an organism that the Constitution grows and changes, and reveals its application to the growth and changes in society.

❧ 11 ❧

Jim Crow and the Supreme Court

The about-face by the Supreme Court that has had the most profound effects upon life in the United States is the one delivered on May 17, 1954, in which all nine justices declared that segregation in public schools by race or color is repugnant to the Constitution. The decision marked the beginning of the end of racial discrimination as the law of the land, just as the case overruled that day, *Plessy v. Ferguson*, had marked on May 18, 1896, what Professor C. Vann Woodward of Yale once called the birth of Jim Crow.

If Jim Crow may be said to have been born that day, he was conceived ten years earlier. For more than twenty years after the end of the Civil War, the color line was drawn only by private persons or groups. In parts of the South the races mingled with a freedom that has not been known since in most places, North or South.

Supreme Court decisions in the early 1880s declared the courts powerless to prevent discrimination in the private sector, since the Fourteenth Amendment was directed solely at the states. Then in 1887 Florida adopted a law requiring railroads to carry Negroes and whites in separate cars or compartments. Other Southern states followed suit. Segregated schools also became a custom. Congress itself, still full of the Radical Republicans who had guided Reconstruction, set up separate black and white schools for the District of Columbia.

The racial law destined to be tested was a Louisiana statute passed in 1890 by a legislature that contained enough black members to have blocked it. They would have had to withhold their votes from a lottery bill until the lottery company, which then virtually owned the legislature, ordered its minions to drop the transportation proposal.

However, the company had bought most of the Negro legislators, too, so the measure requiring railroads to provide separate but equal accommodations for the two races went through. Exempted from its provisions were black nurses of white children; they could ride with their charges in the white coaches.

The Negro population of the United States in 1890 was 7,489,000, ten times the number counted in the first census of 1790. Blacks had then constituted nearly 20 percent of the total; by 1890 blacks constituted less than 15 percent and were still declining in proportion, partly because of white immigration and partly because the Negro death rate was higher than that of whites. At the outbreak of the Civil War, 90 percent of the blacks had been slaves. Forty years later almost the same percentage continued to live in the old slave states, bound to the plantations by sharecropping almost as effectively as they had been by slavery.

In other than racial matters, by the time the Supreme Court heard the case in 1896, a certain innocence prevailed. No one had yet been killed in a motor car accident and the first automobile advertisement was two years away. The first personal injury took place in 1896, though, and the driver of the car, which hit a bicyclist and broke her leg, spent the night in jail.

Louisiana at that time had a larger proportion of well-educated and well-to-do Negroes than any other state. The French and Spanish heritage had made New Orleans singularly free from racial prejudice for an American city. This continued until the growing political strength of the lower-caste whites after Reconstruction led the more successful elected officials to embrace Jim Crow as their own.

In New Orleans, a group of Negro leaders organized a committee to fight the separate-but-equal law through the courts. Railroad officials were sympathetic and helpful, some because they did not like the law on moral grounds, others because they hoped to avoid the expense of extra cars.

A member of the committee got himself arrested for sitting in a white coach on a trip from New Orleans to Mobile. Before he could be tried, the state supreme court ruled that the law could not apply to interstate passengers, since that was an area reserved for Congress.

The committee consulted counsel, and on June 7, 1892, Homer Adolph Plessy sat down in a car reserved for whites on the East Louisiana Railroad for a ride wholly within the state. Since he was lighter in color than a good many of his fellow passengers—one-eighth African blood, which "is not discernible," he later testified—arrangements had been made in advance for Detective Christopher Cain to arrest him and charge him with violation of the segregation law.

The committee had hired a former carpetbagger named Albion Tourgée of Mayville, New York, to conduct Plessy's defense and test the law. Tourgée had been one of the more respectable Northerners who had presided over Southern Reconstruction.

A lawyer of considerable reputation, he had served with distinction in a superior court in North Carolina for six years. He had been instrumental in selecting Plessy for the test case because he had a theory of defense that involved a plea for a nearly-white Negro.

He started by asking Judge John H. Ferguson of the criminal district court to rule the Louisiana statute unconstitutional. The judge refused, and an appeal was taken to the state supreme court against his decision, so that the case became for the record *Plessy v. Ferguson*. The state's highest court was headed by a man who as governor had signed the 1890 separate-but-equal law. As Tourgée and the committee had expected, the judges early in 1893 affirmed Ferguson's decision. They found "the dissatisfaction . . . so unreasonable that we can account for it only on the ground of some misconception."

"Even were it true," they said, "that the statute is prompted by prejudice on the part of one race to be thrown in such contact with the other, one would suppose that to be a sufficient reason why the pride and self-respect of the other race should equally prompt it to avoid such contact if it could be done without the sacrifice of equal accommodations."

Such an expression in what had been the heart of racial toleration perhaps explains why, by the time the Supreme Court in Washington heard Plessy's final appeal two and a half years later, Jim Crow had made great strides. Congress repealed most of the Reconstruction civil rights acts in 1894.

The most distinguished Negro leader, Booker T. Washington, delivered a speech in Atlanta that was taken by most whites and many blacks to mean that Negroes should accept a subordinate position in American society. They could then feel, as many did years later during Teddy Roosevelt's Administration, that for

Washington to dine in the White House was a great step forward.

When the 1896 term of the Supreme Court, which handed down so many of the decisions that were later overruled, took up *Plessy v. Ferguson*, the justices listened to virtually every legal argument against "separate but equal" that would be presented in the 1950s. They also heard one that was not offered later—that Plessy's arrest had unconstitutionally deprived him of his most valuable property, said property being a belief by others that he was white.

The point seems rather oddly taken on behalf of a man who had gone to a good deal of trouble to identify himself as sufficiently black to be arrested for sitting in a white coach. But Tourgée wanted to bear down on the humiliation and deprivations that state-enforced segregation causes.

This ploy gave him an opportunity to answer the Louisiana court's complacency by pointing out that the degradation of the black was such that most white men would prefer death to living as a Negro in the United States. Tourgée went on to say the law was intended to debase blacks solely to gratify feelings of white superiority, as the exemption of nurses tending white children proved. He denied the state had any right to label one person white and another colored "in the common enjoyment of a public highway," and he introduced an often-quoted metaphor:

"Justice is pictured as blind, and her daughter, the law, ought at least to be color-blind."

Generations of lawyers have admired Tourgée's brief, but at the time only one justice, John Marshall Harlan, the former slaveowner who had become the Court's chief champion of equality for blacks, agreed with the argument. Justice Brewer took no part, and the seven others spoke through Justice Brown to validate state-imposed social or educational segregation of people on the basis of color.

The Court, the same as that which dealt with the income tax cases the year before except for Jackson, who had been replaced by

Peckham, more accurately mirrored white public opinion of the day on race than on money. It is very doubtful that as many as one out of nine of the country's 60 million whites stood for genuine equality. That, of course, takes no account of nearly one-eighth of the population, for in 1896 the country had about 8 million blacks. (The Negro proportion declined during the next sixty years.)

Justice Brown's opinion started from the premise that color is a reasonable basis for segregation. From that, he deduced that Jim Crow laws are constitutional as an exercise of the police power to preserve peace and order, that "separation [of the races] in places where they are liable to be brought in contact does not necessarily imply the inferiority of either," that laws can never "eradicate racial instincts or . . . abolish distinctions based upon physical differences," and that the Fourteenth Amendment intended no more than what he vaguely called "the absolute equality of the two races before the law."

Since Plessy was asking for equality of transportation before the law and had legally been excluded from a white coach, "separate" could constitutionally include "equal." Furthermore, Brown added, the authority of the states to enforce segregation was "generally, if not universally, recognized."

"The most common instance of this," he said, is connected with the establishment of separate schools for white and colored children, which have been held to be a valid exercise of the legislative power even by courts of states where the political rights of the colored race have been longest and most earnestly enforced."

He cited a long list of state court decisions to that effect, and referred to the uncontested establishment of Jim Crow schools in the District of Columbia by the Congress itself. He reverted to the thesis that the police power must be unquestioned as long as it is exercised "reasonably," and since racial segregation is inherently reasonable, the Louisiana courts' ruling must be affirmed.

Justice Harlan wrote a passionate dissent that became one of the foundations of the later overruling. He considered separation a "badge of servitude. It cannot be justified on any legal grounds."

He adopted a phrase of Tourgée's but altered it to say that the Constitution is color-blind. He ridiculed the idea that Jim Crow laws were no reflection on any group, and he became prophetic as well as poetic:

> The destinies of the two races in this country are indissolubly linked together, and the interests of both require that the common government of all shall not permit the seeds of race hate to be planted under the sanction of law. . . . We boast of the freedom enjoyed by our people above all other peoples. But it is difficult to reconcile that boast with a state of law which, practically, puts the brand of servitude and degradation upon a large class of our fellow citizens—our equals before the law. The thin disguise of 'equal' accommodations for passengers in railroad coaches will not mislead anyone, nor atone for the wrong this day done. . . . The present decision, it may well be apprehended, will not only stimulate aggressions more or less brutal and irritating, upon the admitted rights of colored citizens, but will encourage the belief that it is possible, by means of state enactments, to defeat the beneficent purposes which the people of the United States had in view when they adopted the recent amendments of the Constitution. . . . In my opinion, the judgment this day rendered will, in time, prove to be quite as pernicious as the decision made by this tribunal in the Dred Scott Case.

Harlan's prophecy was amply fulfilled. *Plessy v. Ferguson* was cited successfully in defense of progressively more rigid barriers against Negroes—in jobs as well as schools, on streetcars and buses, in theaters and restaurants, waiting rooms and washrooms, in the armed forces, even in courtrooms and on juries. "Separate but equal" justified any form of segregation, although hardly anywhere was more than lip service paid to "equal."

Schools and other facilities for Negroes were notoriously inferior and sedulously kept that way. During the next fifty years, little evidence of white revulsion against legally enforced segregation can be discerned. Lynchings, the brutalities of chain gangs, and the more outrageous denials of the vote provoked popular indignation from time to time, but that was all.

In 1950, it is safe to say, the overwhelming masses of white Americans were quite tolerant of the racial status quo, and foreign observers marveled at the apparent submissiveness of blacks. Population had more than doubled since 1896, to 151 million, thanks in part to immigration, but the Negro numbers had not increased as fast, standing at about 15 million. At the same time, the "knowledge explosion" was in full swing, radically altering the outlook of everyone exposed to it. It is estimated that it took man 1,750 years to double his knowledge after the beginning of the Christian era, especially scientific and technical knowledge. But he doubled it again between 1750 and 1900, again by 1950, and was rushing ahead at such a pace that the next doubling required only fifteen years.

Under the circumstances, the value of an education became obvious even to unlettered and uninformed Americans. With only slight exaggeration it began to be said that a boy couldn't get a job as a shipping clerk without a college degree. The substandard character of most Negro schools became more galling the more education seemed to have value.

By 1952, the Supreme Court had insisted six times that states must enforce "equal" in higher education, even if it meant giving up "separate." All the decisions affected graduate schools, however, and no one else. In one case, the Court ruled that Texas must let a qualified Negro into its state university law school rather than keep him in an inferior school for blacks only. Missouri was forbidden to dodge the rule by sending a Negro to an out-of-state law school; the Court said a degree granted in the state where a lawyer is to practice has advantages. Oklahoma was ordered to cease segregating its lone black law student in classes, dining hall, and library. The Court reached these decisions without having to confront *Plessy v. Ferguson* head on.

The easy solution was no longer possible, as a report by President Truman's Civil Rights Commission pointed out in 1948. This became clearer when the validity of segregated public schools reached the Court in 1952. The case that drew the main opinion was *Oliver Brown* et al. *v. Board of Education of Topeka* et al. Four others had been joined with it for decision, each affecting black children of a different school system. There were five youngsters in whose names and on whose behalf the suits had been brought: Linda Brown, eleven years old, Oliver's daughter, who had been barred from an elementary school five blocks from her home and forced to take a bus—she had to cross a railroad yard to get to the bus stop—to an all-black school twenty blocks further. Ethel Belton, seventeen, was not allowed to attend the high school in Claymont, Delaware, where she lived, and rode forty-five minutes by bus each way to a Negro high school in Wilmington. The name of Harry Briggs, Jr., thirteen, appeared in the title of his case because it was the first alphabetically on a list of sixty-seven children in Summerton, South Carolina, whose parents were suing to integrate the schools. Dorothy Davis, a seventeen-year-old, had been disciplined for taking part in a pupil strike against conditions in the black schools in Prince Edward County, Virginia. Spottswood Bollings, fifteen, had been refused admission to a new high school in Washington, D.C., because it was reserved for whites; he was the only one for whom the protection of the Fourteenth Amendment could not be pleaded since the wrong against him had been committed by Congress, so he sued under the Fifth.

Both sides had the benefit of highly regarded advocates. Thurgood Marshall, counsel for the National Association for the Advancement of Colored People, and destined to be the Court's first

Negro justice, presented the case for the children, drawing heavily upon Tourgée's 1896 brief and Harlan's dissent in *Plessy*. He was answered by John W. Davis, head of one of the country's most prestigious law firms, who had run for President in 1924 and once refused a Supreme Court nomination. At the end of the argument, the Court wanted to know more about the circumstances surrounding the adoption of the Fourteenth Amendment so far as these applied to education. It was by no means clear that those who drafted the Amendment's two key sentences had intended to abolish or forbid segregation in the schools. Chief Justice Vinson, therefore, set reargument for December 8, 1953.

He died a few months before that date at the age of sixty-three, very young for a judge of the highest court, and President Eisenhower appointed Earl Warren, who had served as Attorney General and Governor of California—he had submitted a brief defending the state's right to bar indigents in *Edwards v. California*—and was generally regarded as a safe, middle-of-the-road Republican. He had been well enough thought of by all wings of the party to be nominated for Vice-President in 1948. Warren took his seat at the opening of the term when the school segregation issue was to be reargued.

The delay served chiefly to let the decision be recorded for the Warren rather than the Vinson Court, since precious little information about any educational intentions that may have been back of the Fourteenth Amendment had been uncovered. Apparently the framers did not think about that subject at all.

At the time of its adoption, 1868, the South had no public schools for whites, let alone blacks. Some private charity schools for white children were maintained, as in the North, by religious groups. Only a few Northern states, led by Massachusetts in 1852, had compulsory education laws and none had a free public high school system.

Over much of the country that did have public schools, they were open for three months a year. The one significant fact researchers turned up in the realm of law, so far as schooling went, was that a number of Southern states had operated for years under statutes that prohibited teaching Negroes to read and write.

When the Fourteenth Amendment was ratified, the impeachment trial of President Johnson had just ended with his acquittal. The United States had acquired Alaska and was preparing to elect General Grant to the Presidency. Congress had established the Office of Education, reorganized from a Department of Education created the year before. Such things as a university chair of education, honors courses, women Ph.D.s, county or rural high schools, and college summer schools were as yet unknown, but this year the country saw its first kindergarten and first commercial high school.

No hints of how the rearguments and their own studies and discussions affected their judgment escaped the nine judges. The Supreme Court is the only leakproof ship of state we have, and it takes excellent care to remain that way. The weekly conferences at which, in Jefferson's indignant phrase, "an opinion is huddled up in conclave," are inviolably secret. No one ever is admitted to the room except the justices themselves. The traditional duty of the junior member is to guard the door, answer any knock, and take the message. Equally inviolable is the rule that justices do not reveal any of the give and take around the table, although it is clear from the occasional vehemence of a dissent that heated dialogue is not unknown. Before the Court got its own printing shop, several typesetters were used to prepare different sections of the opinions so that no one would know the full text in advance of the Court's release.

The school cases had aroused interest, of course, but comments published while the Court deliberated suggest that few anticipated any far-reaching results. Perhaps the majority would issue some stern rules that Negro schools really must meet the same academic standards as white schools in the same community, while Black and Douglas would urge more.

On Monday morning, May 17, 1954, the pressroom downstairs in the Supreme Court Building buzzed with talk, but not about law. This was the eighteenth day of the Army-McCarthy hearings, the running drama that was the beginning of the end of the Wisconsin Senator's Red witch-hunt and of his own career.

Shortly after noon, a Court attaché interrupted newsmen's speculations on what was coming next in the hearings to advise them they could learn something of interest in the courtroom. Some of them immediately recognized the significance of a more than usually distinguished audience and of the presence on the bench of Justice Jackson, who had left a sickbed so that the rule announced this day would have the obvious personal support of the whole Court. They were an unusually experienced group; all except Warren had served from five to seventeen years.

The new Chief Justice began reading shortly before one o'clock, and even after he was well along in his opinion for a unanimous Court, the conclusion was not obvious. At 1:12 P.M. an Associated Press bulletin announced that an attack on segregation was underway, but it was too early to say just what it would be.

At about the time this bulletin was composed, the reader had probably reached the passage in which he commented on the paucity of evidence that those who were responsible for adoption of the Fourteenth Amendment in 1868 had considered the schools.

"As a consequence," he said, "it is not surprising that there should be so little in the history of the Fourteenth Amendment relating to the intended effect on public education."

On the other hand, he and his colleagues had no dearth of information on the role of education today and the effect of segregation upon the victims of it, both black and white.

Warren's opinion deals with these points so elaborately that he was accused of writing a sociological tract instead of a judicial opinion.

Actually, the Court was faced, as it had been often before, with the necessity of applying constitutional principles to situations that were impossible and unpredictable when the words the judges must construe were written. Even when the intentions of the men who wrote the words was clear, it might not help much. For example, Thaddeus Stevens, the Radical Republican leader who had introduced the Amendment and led the forces that obtained its ratification, made his intentions perfectly plain. He said frankly that the Amendment was designed to win votes for his party. He was also a firm, sincere believer in complete racial equality, but even an approximate estimate of how many who voted for ratification agreed with him is impossible to arrive at. So in 1954, the nine justices in their conference room and at their own desks had wrestled with the meaning of "equal protection of the laws" in modern society.

"In approaching this problem," they explained through their Chief, "we cannot turn the clock back to 1868 when the Amendment was adopted, or even to 1896 when *Plessy v. Ferguson* was written. We must consider public education in the light of its full development and its present place in American life throughout the Nation."

The opinion emphasized the changes that had taken place in the world, and especially in the world of learning. In 1868, the low priority that public officials accorded to schools was understandable, for bare literacy was as much as most people could use or expect. "Today," Warren pointed out, "education is perhaps the most important function of state and local government. . . . In these days, it is doubtful that any child can reasonably be expected to succeed in life if he is denied the opportunity of an education." The first decisive question for the Court to decide, therefore, and the answer to it were:

"Does segregation of children in public schools solely on the basis of race, even though the physical facilities and other 'tangible' factors may be equal, deprive the children of the minority group of equal educational opportunities? We believe that it does."

The evidence by modern psychologists and social scientists,

although not contained in buckram-bound volumes of the law, was overwhelming in support of this position, and Warren cited a good deal of it. He also had some judicial authority for the conclusion that even equal tangible facilities may not offer equal educational opportunity. The Supreme Court itself, ordering Missouri to admit a Negro to the state university law school, mentioned "those qualities which are incapable of objective measurement but which make for greatness in a law school." More to the point, although coming from a less august source, was this statement from the Kansas court in the very ruling from which Oliver Brown was appealing on behalf of his daughter:

> Segregation of white and colored children in public schools has a detrimental effect upon the colored children. The impact is greater when it has the sanction of the law; for the policy of separating the races is usually interpreted by denoting the inferiority of the negro group. A sense of inferiority affects the motivation of the children to learn.

Nevertheless, the Kansas court could find no relief for Linda Brown in the United States Constitution. The Supreme Court had never construed the Fourteenth Amendment's "equal protection of the laws" as reaching so far into matters reserved to the states by the Tenth that Federal courts could pronounce judgment on children's admission to or exclusion from any particular school. *Plessy v. Ferguson* and all the decisions since had commanded only equality, but had never outlawed segregation.

The nine men in Washington knew this quite as well as did the judges in Kansas. But they were in a position to do something about it. Not one of them was prepared to say that a substantive evil can be irremediable under the Constitution. All—Southerners and Northerners, conservatives and liberals—agreed that school segregation is evil. So they were able to answer the other key question in this case: If segregation deprives children of equal educational opportunities, does the Constitution permit the United States courts to end it? Their answer was:

> We conclude that in the field of public education the doctrine of "separate but equal" has no place. Separate educational facilities are inherently unequal. Therefore, we hold that the plaintiffs and others similarly situated for whom the actions have been brought are, by reason of the segregation complained of, deprived of the equal protection of the laws guaranteed by the Fourteenth Amendment. This disposition makes unnecessary any discussion whether such segregation also violates the Due Process Clause of the Fifth Amendment.

But they had been obliged to discuss the similar clause in the Fifth. The problem of their Washington neighbor, Spottswood Bolling, could not be solved by the Fourteenth, since it applies only to the states. So when the Chief Justice finished reading the *Brown* opinion, he took up racial segregation in the District of Columbia schools. It was, he ruled, with all his colleagues concurring, a denial of due process to keep the boy out of a white high school only because he was black.

"Liberty under law," this opinion declared, "extends to the full range of conduct which the individual is free to pursue, and it cannot be restricted except for a proper governmental objective."

The Chief Justice had taken twenty-eight minutes to read the *Brown* opinion. While it was generally realized that the Court had ended lawful segregation in seventeen states and in the District of Columbia, which required it, and in four, including Kansas, which permitted it, the full impact was not so speedily grasped. *Newsweek* was not alone in thinking that the Army-McCarthy hearings rated higher billing than the school decisions. Yet Jim Crow as an officer of the state had been dealt a mortal blow. Warren had not specifically pronounced *Plessy v. Ferguson* overruled—that was to come three years later. But the reasoning behind the ruling and the Court's unanimity clearly foreshadowed future outlawing of segregation in transportation, in public accommodations and facilities of all kinds, in government—in short in all aspects of American society upon which the courts are competent to act.

Brown v. Board of Education did even more than alter forever the relations between blacks and whites in the United States. It announced as clearly as if the opinion had spelled out the words that the Supreme Court had embarked upon a new era. It would be an activist Court. It would reexamine to an even greater extent than its predecessors had done those precedents that the pace of modern life was rendering obsolete. Many people who did not like the pace blamed the judges for it. "Impeach Earl Warren!" was a popular battle cry of some extremists. Yet, as we watch the Warren Court exercise another about-face or two in the next chapter, it should become clear that the motivating force was the rapidity of economic and technological change rather than the revolutionary fervor of judges.

❦ 12 ❦

The Court on Crime and Sex

The reputation of the Supreme Court in the late 1950s and '60s was summed up in a jest that circulated in Justice Black's home state of Alabama. People there remembered that early in his political career and long before he was nominated for the bench he had been a member of the Ku Klux Klan.

"Hugo Black," they said, "used to go around in white robes scaring black people. Now he goes around in black robes scaring white people."

What came to scare a lot of white people more than the Warren Court majority's overruling of racial precedents was the about-face it gave to the handling of suspected criminals in police stations and courts. The major decisions overruling past opinions concerned the admissibility of confessions, conditions under which police may search people and premises, the legality of wiretapping and eavesdropping, and the right of those accused of crime to be represented by a lawyer. On all except wiretapping, a possibility unknown to the men who wrote the Constitution and the Fourteenth Amendment, the Bill of Rights is quite a direction marker. Rules incorporating the safeguards into the practice in Federal cases antedated the Warren Court. The question to be settled now was whether the Fourteenth Amendment bound the states to abide by the protections that the Bill of Rights guaranteed citizens. The debate over this subject had been going on for years, with Black the protagonist for applying the first eight amendments to the states as literally and completely as to the Federal Government, and Frankfurter preferring to permit the states to be their own moral judges. In the past, the latter view had been accepted usually, but the Court for some time had been incorporating more and more of the protection of the Bill of Rights into local law enforcement. The effect was to extend to the less affluent segments of society legal safeguards always enjoyed by the rich.

In 1932, in the case of the "Scottsboro boys," Negroes sentenced to death for allegedly raping two white prostitutes in a freight car after throwing the girls' white companions off the train during a scuffle, the Court held that the Fourteenth Amendment would not let Alabama convict these ignorant illiterates without allowing them a lawyer for their defense. In 1936, in *Brown v. Mississippi*, the Court ruled that a confession extracted from a black man while police had him hanging from a tree was, in the absence of any other evidence of guilt, not a permissible basis for a court-imposed death sentence. Chief Justice Hughes said of this procedure:

"The rack and torture chamber may not be substituted for the witness stand. The State may not permit an accused to be hurried to conviction—where the whole proceeding is but a mask—without supplying corrective procedure."

But before the Warren Court, only the more outrageous state criminal convictions had been reversed. The usual line was that enunciated in 1937 in a case called *Palko v. Connecticut*, in which Justice Cardozo gave the opinion of the Court. The Fourteenth Amendment, he ruled, did not bind the states to such Bill of Rights niceties in dealing with criminals as indictment by a grand jury, trial by a petit jury, or prohibition against double jeopardy, third-degree tactics, and illegal searches. Frank Palko had been found guilty of second-degree murder and sentenced to life imprisonment. The state asked for and got a new trial, at which Palko was convicted of first-degree murder and sentenced to death. Cardozo's view of what states could consider fair was reaffirmed in 1946 in *Adamson v. California*. At this time, Black and Frankfurter explained their respective views at length, with Frankfurter voicing the opinion of the majority.

The public's view on how criminals should be treated has been a slow evolution from supporting the death penalty for offenses that would now be considered mere misdemeanors through the milder extraction of confessions by torture and application of "an eye for an eye" mode of sentencing to the modern argument over whether deterrent or rehabilitation is the proper aim of law enforcement. The theory of reform is older than the practice. The first society organized to remodel prisons was founded in Philadelphia in 1787; the first state-sponsored reformatory for juvenile delinquents opened in New York in 1825—with twice as many girls as boys. But only the most outrageous examples of brutality or denial of fundamental rights ever aroused the public. In this area, courts were consistently ahead of public opinion, and higher courts were more inclined to step further ahead than lower courts.

One of the Warren Court's changes in the criminal field came in 1961 when by 6 to 3 it reversed a 1949 decision that the

Fourteenth Amendment did not oblige Colorado to exclude illegally gathered evidence, although exclusion was the rule in
Federal courts. The rationale was that the lawlessness of an
improper search or wiretap or brutal treatment was committed by
an individual policeman or prosecutor, who should be punished,
but society should not be the loser by releasing a criminal. At least
the states should be free to make up their own rules on that.

The overruling of *Wolf v. Colorado*, as this case was titled,
began on a May morning in 1957 when three Cleveland
policemen received a tip, so they said later, that they would find
gambling equipment and a man wanted for questioning in a
bombing in the home of Dollree Mapp on the second floor of a
two-family house. She refused to let them in without a warrant, on
the advice of her lawyer, whom she called because she was involved in civil litigation. After three hours, reinforcements of four
more policemen arrived, and they broke down the door. One
waved a piece of paper when Miss Mapp demanded to see their
warrant. She grabbed it but before she could learn what it was,
they handcuffed her after a struggle and retrieved it. They found
no trace of the man or the equipment, but in a suitcase in the
basement they came across four pamphlets, two photographs, and
"a little pencil doodle" that they and a judge later called obscene.
Miss Mapp was convicted of possessing pornography, for while the
trial court conceded that the police probably had no warrant, and
the prosecution did not say they did, the evidence had not been
taken from the woman's person by "the use of brutal or offensive
physical force." This the police employed only to get back the
pretended warrant, so *Wolf v. Colorado* could apply.

When the case reached the Supreme Court on appeal in 1961,
Miss Mapp's counsel asked that her conviction be reversed on the
grounds both of an illegal search and of the constitutional invalidity
of Ohio's statute making it a crime to have obscene items for one's
own pleasure. The Court, speaking through Justice Clark,
declined to go into the question of pornography at all. It was

unnecessary since Miss Mapp should go free because the 1949 ruling had been based on a mistaken interpretation of the Fourteenth Amendment.

"We hold that all evidence obtained by searches and seizures in violation of the Constitution is, by that same authority, inadmissible in a state court," Clark wrote.

The majority eased the about-face for those who still said it was no business of the Supreme Court to supervise such procedures in state courts by noting that most states had adopted the exclusion rule since 1949—although not Ohio. The reason usually given was that this was the only remedy for police lawlessness. The Court held it was time for all to follow the same procedure. Justice Black, who had been in the *Wolf* majority, and also in this one, delivered a concurring opinion to explain why he had changed his mind. He now believed that the Fifth Amendment protection against self-incrimination applied, since the fruit of the illegal search was the suspect's own papers and possessions.

Two years later, the Court went back a few years more to overrule *Betts v. Brady*, decided in 1942. In that, the justices had refused to extend to poor people accused of non-capital crimes the right of counsel so eloquently demanded for the "Scottsboro boys." Betts, a farm hand out of a job, had been convicted of robbery in Carroll County, Maryland, after being obliged to conduct his own defense before a judge without a jury. He had asked the court to appoint a lawyer to help him because he was too poor to hire one. The judge replied that only suspects accused of rape or murder had this privilege. Betts's plea to upset his eight-year sentence reached the Supreme Court as a suit against the warden, Brady. Justice Roberts for the Court held that states did not have to provide counsel in all trials, even of defendants accused of serious offenses, saying:

That which may, in one setting, constitute a denial of fundamental fairness, shocking to the universal sense of justice, may, in other circumstances, and in the light of other considerations, fall short of such denial.

The majority was willing to let the state courts decide what constitutes "fundamental fairness" in this matter of counsel. Justice Black, joined by Douglas and Murphy, dissented, because they thought the Sixth Amendment clause, "In all criminal prosecutions, the accused shall enjoy the right . . . to have the assistance of counsel for his defense," was made binding upon state as well as Federal courts by the Fourteenth Amendment. Twenty-one years later, on March 18, 1963, Black had the satisfaction of converting his dissent into the law of the land. He read the opinion of the Court on the appeal of Clarence Earl Gideon, who was suing Warden Wainwright of Florida to get out of jail, where he was confined for five years for breaking into a poolroom with intent to commit a misdemeanor. He had asked his trial judge to assign a defense lawyer. When the judge replied that he was sorry but only indigents accused of capital crimes could have free legal aid in Florida, Gideon had cried out: "The United States Supreme Court says I am entitled to be represented by counsel."

He was a bit premature, but when he got his case to Washington, the Court lived up to its principles by assigning him a lawyer, which, as Justice Clark noted in the very next case decided, was rarely done in those august premises. It was very high-powered talent that the Court appointed, too, to plead Gideon's case—Abe Fortas, head of a leading Washington law firm, adviser to Presidents, and within two years to occupy a seat on the Supreme Court himself. The Justices also told the counsel the main point they were to argue: "Should this Court's holding in *Betts v. Brady* . . . be overruled?" The judges were treated to an unusually extensive debate. Two states appealed in support of Florida, urging that *Betts* be upheld. Twenty-eight states, as "friends of the court," contended that *Betts* should be overruled.

"We agree," Black concluded his opinion, after referring to this preponderance of distaste for the *Betts* ruling. He took notice of the fact that Gideon had conducted his defense "about as well" as any layman could be expected to do, with an opening statement, cross-examination of prosecution witnesses, presentation of his own, and a brief closing argument in which he protested his innocence instead of taking the stand. But, Black observed, he did not know how to make use of the "procedural and substantive safeguards" that someone trained in the law can employ, which is why defendants who are not indigent often hire the best lawyers they can afford. He quoted with approval Justice Sutherland's opinion in the *Scottsboro* case, "The right to be heard would be, in many cases, of little avail if it did not comprehend the right to counsel." Black thought this a better rule than *Betts*, although Sutherland had limited its application to the case before the Court.

All eight of Black's colleagues agreed with him in preferring the *Scottsboro* rule to *Betts*, but one concurred only in part. This one was a second John Marshall Harlan, grandson of the great dissenter of the late nineteenth century. As Federal appeals court judge in New York, he had been appointed in 1955 to succeed Jackson. He now wrote a separate opinion to say Gideon should have had a lawyer, but also to protest mildly, "I agree that *Betts v. Brady* should be overruled, but consider it entitled to a more respectful burial than has been accorded, at least on the part of those who were not on the Court when that case was decided."

Now that we have *Gideon* for a precedent, the trend is toward state-appointed lawyers to represent indigents in civil lawsuits.

In popular interest and popular imagination, the question of counsel for the poor in criminal cases was overshadowed in the same year as the Gideon case by the Court's opinion about Danny Escobedo, a twenty-two-year-old of Mexican extraction convicted in Chicago of murdering his brother-in-law. The chief evidence against him was a confession he made after long sessions of questioning by the police, who kept telling him he would help himself if he told the truth, since they had plenty on him to get a conviction, which was not true. The young man, poorly educated and obviously uninformed about the technicalities of arrest procedures, wanted to consult his lawyer, but this was refused. No one told him he had a right to remain silent. At his trial, his incriminating statements were read to the jury, admitted on the strength of a long line of Supreme Court decisions going back to 1908. The settled view had been expressed by Justice Cardozo in 1937 in *Palko v. Connecticut*. As has been noted, Cardozo found this to be constitutional within a theory that the Supreme Court ought not to police the state tribunals but rather vest in them responsibility and discretion in maintaining justice. What he suggested was a selective application of the Bill of Rights to the states on a fairly flexible basis.

When Escobedo's appeal was reached shortly after Gideon's, Arthur Goldberg, the Secretary of Labor, had taken Frankfurter's seat, and he wrote the opinion of a court divided 5 to 4 in reversing the conviction—it almost certainly would have been 5 to 4 the other way if Frankfurter had not resigned. Goldberg took up the argument that if a prisoner knew his rights and immediately got a lawyer to help, the police would get no confessions, because any attorney worth his salt would command his client to keep quiet. The Justice answered that the very argument shows this is the stage where a suspect needs to know his rights. Furthermore, the Constitution is on his side.

"We have learned the lesson of history, ancient and modern," he said, "that a system of criminal law enforcement which comes to depend on the 'confession' will, in the long run, be less reliable and more subject to abuses than a system which depends on extrinsic evidence independently secured through skillful investigation."

Another newcomer on the Court, Byron R. White, wrote a dissent in which he clearly implied the majority was making law, not interpreting it. The Constitution only forbids the authorities to "compel" anyone to incriminate himself, White pointed out. All forms of non-compulsory questioning, therefore, are within the discretion of the states. They could make such rules as the Court now laid down, but justices should not. White thought the majority opinion "reflects a deep-seated distrust of law enforcement officers everywhere," which he did not share. Nevertheless, confessions obtained without meticulous regard for the suspect's rights were no longer valid evidence, and *Palko* and all the other precedents to the contrary were overruled.

In 1966, the Court carried this a step further, apparently in an effort to clarify the standards it had set up in *Escobedo*. By this time Abe Fortas, Gideon's lawyer, had replaced Goldberg, who resigned to become Ambassador to the United Nations. The case was the appeal of Ernesto Miranda, convicted of kidnapping and rape in Arizona. He had been arrested at his home and questioned by two policemen. He was informed that he need say nothing, and if he did his words could be used against him. He was not told he had a right to a lawyer, and he did not ask for one. After about two hours—no brutality or harshness was alleged—Miranda signed a confession.

Warren, writing for another 5 to 4 majority, noted that "the indigent Mexican defendant was a seriously disturbed individual with pronounced sexual fantasies." The interrogation, "psychologically rather than physically oriented," while he was kept incommunicado, "is at odds with one of our Nation's most cherished principles—that the individual may not be compelled to incriminate himself." So it is not enough to allow a suspect to call a lawyer. He must be told before any questioning is attempted that he may do so, and the rest of the prescribed warning must be stated clearly, including the fact that if he can't afford a lawyer, the state will provide one. Warren added that the Court had re-examined *Escobedo* thoroughly, "and we reaffirm it."

Justice Clark concurred in part and dissented in part. Three other justices dissented even more outspokenly than in *Escobedo*,

Harlan, for example, calling the decision "poor constitutional law" and predicting "harmful consequences for the country at large."

For all the anguished outcry from some prosecutors and policemen, and a provision in a 1968 act of Congress to modify the *Miranda* rule, it remains in force because of fear that in a test, the Court would find the 1968 statute unconstitutional. Besides, other law enforcement experts think the safeguards of the accused, affecting as they do only a tiny fraction of those arrested, are always sound practice. Even with *Miranda*, the great majority of all penal cases end in a plea of guilty, and usually the trial starts that way.

Privacy, as a legal right, is virtually an American invention, and a fairly recent one. Louis D. Brandeis, early in his law practice, and his then partner, Charles Warren, first stated the principle in a *Harvard Law Review* article in 1890. Their discovery that man is entitled to be let alone stemmed from their outrage over sensational newspaper ac:ounts of Boston bluebloods, of whom Warren was one. Since then, the sophistication of eavesdropping technology is such that people can be overheard from a distance without necessarily planting "bugs" or tapping wires. Next step? Possibly electronic snooping inside the brain so that even our thoughts may be made available to anyone with curiosity and a sensitive machine. What the Supreme Court has said about these matters may prove to be prologue to the tale of our surviving freedoms.

Linked to the problem of the confession extorted or freely given at the police station has been the evidence acquired through illegal eavesdropping or wiretapping. This has been a controversial issue ever since skilled mechanics learned how to listen in on a telephone line. In justification, tappers have said it is no worse than overhearing a conversation between two crooks while standing outside an open window. Defenders of privacy reply that people can close the window, but have no way of closing off the telephone.

The landmark case that failed to settle the issue long before the Warren Court concerned a rum runner named Olmstead, head of a large, Seattle-based operation. He was convicted during Prohibition on the evidence of 775 pages of conversation Federal agents heard in the five months they tapped his telephone. In 1928, Chief Justice Taft spoke for a majority of five and Justices Holmes and Brandeis for the four dissenters. Among them they gave the substance of most arguments on the subject. The principal changes time has brought have been increasing sophistication of devices for snooping that approach listening to a man's thoughts.

Taft's basic rationale for upholding official tapping was that no physical trespass on the property of the defendant was involved. Holmes objected mainly because this was "dirty business," and he held it "a less evil that some criminals should escape than that the government should play an ignoble part." Brandeis went into detail concerning the changes in communications that technology was bringing about. He warned that the law must keep up with them. The wiretap, he said, is more effective than thumbscrew and rack "to obtain disclosure in court of what is whispered in the closet." More than thirty years earlier, Brandeis with his then law partner had virtually invented the law of privacy, and he recognized the grave threat the future electronic eavesdropping portended, not just to criminals but to anyone the authorities disliked or distrusted.

Congress tried to overrule the *Olmstead* decision in 1934 by forbidding the interception, divulgence or publication of any wire communication. This meant policemen should get a judge's permission to plant a tap, to be given only after a showing of cause in the same way as a search warrant is issued. But Congress said nothing about evidence that policemen obtained by violating the rules. So *Olmstead* remained law so far as letting juries hear overheard conversations.

Debate over the "dirty business" continued with rising intensity, and one of its peaks came in 1967 in what is known to the press as "the Playboy Club Case" and to the courts as *Berger v. New York*. In the course of an investigation as to whether an attempt had been made to bribe the State Liquor Authority to get a license for a Playboy Club, a judge authorized wiretaps in accordance with state law. As a result, Ralph Berger was convicted of conspiracy to bribe the chairman. While the Supreme Court reversed the conviction, 6 to 3, no clearcut opinion of the Court emerged. Three statements were delivered for the majority and one each for the three minority members. Douglas in the majority and Black in the minority agreed on one point, that *Olmstead* had been overruled. But others in the majority, notably Clark, writing one of his last opinions before he resigned (to be succeeded by Thurgood Marshall) did not say so.

A greater unanimity, although not perfect, prevailed later in the year 1967 when the justices heard the somewhat less complicated case of Charles Katz, whose conversations from a Los Angeles telephone booth were overheard by FBI agents seeking evidence that he was committing the crime of transmitting wagering information across state lines. They got it by means of a "bug" that they rested on top of the booth. The United States district court and circuit court of appeals agreed that this was reasonable in view of the agents' belief that Katz used the booth to telephone bets to Miami. The Supreme Court, with only Black dissenting, said no, suspicion is not enough, and the FBI should get a warrant.

"For the Fourth Amendment protects people, not places," the decision declared. "One who occupies it [the booth], shuts the door behind him, and pays the toll that permits him to place a call is surely entitled to assume that the words he utters into the mouthpiece will not be broadcast to the world. . . . The Government's activities . . . violated the privacy upon which he justifiably relied . . . and thus constituted a 'search and seizure' within the meaning of the Fourth Amendment."

That this settles the matter of eavesdropping and the Constitution is hardly likely. Nearly everyone would allow taps without court orders in national security and kidnapping cases. But law still needs to clarify reasons and procedures involved in all other eavesdropping. When Warren Burger came from the District of Columbia Court of Appeals to take Earl Warren's place in 1969, the question of wiretaps and indeed of the constitutional protections of persons suspected of crimes were hardly solidified into unbreakable moulds. A modification of the standards now required may seem more likely than an actual about-face on any of the issues discussed here. But, as Justice Douglas said in *Gideon*, "Yet, happily, all constitutional questions are always open."

For our final example of Supreme Court overrulings, we come to a case that may mark the about-face pattern of the Burger Court, as *Brown v. Board of Education* did that of its predecessor in 1954. As Chief Justice Warren presided over a bench that struck down legal discrimination against blacks, Chief Justice Burger may be remembered by history for leading the way to reversing laws that discriminate against women. November 22, 1971, may go down with May 17, 1954, as a landmark date in the chronicle of human freedom. For on November 22, in *Reed v. Reed*, a unanimous Court declared that the equal protection clause of the Fourteenth Amendment prohibits a state from decreeing that men shall be preferred over women when the difference in sex bears no rational relationship to the state's objectives.

In a sense, this decision may be said to have overruled several millennia of human history as well as an 1872 opinion of the Court in *Bradwell v. The State*. The 1972 ruling grew out of a new spirit of emancipation that was still a little ahead of its time. Some people even then recognized its relation to the conflict over slavery, for the legal status of women had been the model for the legal status of slaves in this country. A supposed inferiority, by which Negro servitude was justified, was given also as the reason why a woman's property and person belonged to her husband.

Her standing before the law—or lack of it—came to this country with the common law of England. A woman was not competent to testify under canon law, and of course could not serve on a jury, enter the professions, go to college, or even speak in public. When a woman married, she lost all legal identity. Husband and wife were "esteemed but as one Person in Law, and are presumed to have but one Will," as the medieval phrase had it.

The right to speak in public was one of the first barriers to drop—in 1838. After 1848, laws permitting married women to own property in their own names began to be adopted. That same year, the first women's rights convention was held in Seneca Falls, New York, called by Mrs. Elizabeth Cady Stanton. After the Civil War, agitation for suffrage intensified, and Wyoming Territory granted it to women in 1869. The Mormons followed suit in Utah Territory the same year. Already Elizabeth Blackwell had been graduated from a medical school, Geneva College, 1849; Antoinette Brown ordained a minister, 1852; Arabella Mansfield admitted to the practice of law in Iowa, 1869. But in 1872, these examples of escape from bondage no more betokened emancipation than had the occasional Negro success story before the war.

Myra Bradwell of Chicago learned this in 1872 when she presented to the supreme court of Illinois, which licensed lawyers to practice, the customary certificate showing her good character and professional qualifications. The justices turned her down because she was not only a woman but married, and so could not be bound by a contract "nor by those implied contracts which it is the policy of the law to create between attorney and client."

Mrs. Bradwell demanded reasons in writing, and got them. Illinois had by statute adopted the English common law and, with three irrelevant exceptions, the statutes of that country enacted before the fourth year of James I (1607). Female attorneys were unknown in England then, and even at the time Illinois took over the common law the notion of a woman lawyer would have created as much astonishment as a woman member of Parliament (the ultimate in fantasy, apparently).

Furthermore, Mrs. Bradwell was to remember that "God designed the sexes to occupy different spheres of action, and that it belonged to men to make, apply, and execute the laws" was regarded as an almost axiomatic truth. Obviously, when the state legislature gave to the supreme court the power to license lawyers, it did not mean this privilege should extend to women.

Mrs. Bradwell appealed to the Supreme Court in Washington on the ground that the Fourteenth Amendment applied to women as well as blacks. Justice Miller for the Court said this was not so. The immediately preceding case had thrown out an appeal of Louisiana butchers that they were denied due process of law by a slaughterhouse monopoly. These Slaughter House Cases were the first to attempt to extend the Amendment's coverage to anyone except former slaves, and failed by 5 to 4. Mrs. Bradwell failed by 8 to 1. Miller said the same rule governed her case. Bradley, who had dissented in the Slaughter House Cases, concurred now, saying Mrs. Bradwell was excluded from practicing law for better reasons than the ones that kept butchers out of the slaughterhouse, because:

> Man is, or should be, woman's protector and defender. The natural and proper timidity and delicacy which belongs to the female sex evidently unfits it for many of the occupations of civil life.

God and the very nature of things set females in a domestic role, "repugnant to the idea of a woman adopting a distinct and independent career apart from that of her husband."

Miller noted that in most states women were incapable of making a binding contract without their husbands' consent. As for unmarried women, they were exceptions to the general rule and the law of the Creator was that they be wives and mothers.

All this put it within the police power of the state "to ordain what offices, positions, and callings shall be filled and discharged by men, and shall receive the benefits of those energies and responsibilities, and that decision and firmness which are presumed to predominate in the sterner sex."

The lone dissenter, who gave no opinion, was the Chief Justice. He was the parent of Kate Chase Sprague, who was one of the most powerful personalities in Washington and widely believed to have carved out much of her father's career with her own fair hands. She was more than a famous hostess; her political skill was greatly admired, and sometimes feared. Under the circumstances, the Chief Justice could be expected to have a somewhat more enlightened, or perhaps chastened, view of woman's place.

Despite the Supreme Court's verdict, emancipation was on the march when Justice Miller wrote, led by such very different figures as Mrs. Stanton, Susan B. Anthony, and the beautiful swindler, Victoria Woodhull, who was actively running for President, at least in the weekly paper she and her sister published. Progress on the political front was steady. By the time we entered World War I in 1917, eleven states west of the Mississippi had enfranchised women and Illinois permitted them to vote for President. Later that year, New York adopted women's suffrage by referendum. Congress passed the Nineteenth Amendment in 1919, and the necessary thirty-six states ratified it by the summer of 1920, the last one, Tennessee, by the margin of a single vote in the legislature.

Breaking down inequality in employment and pay, jury service, and many other aspects of life proceeded as slowly. By 1970, for example, only twenty-eight states had the same rules for men and women jurors. Despite some equal-pay-for-equal-work laws, most employed women did not benefit from this, although by 1971 more than two out of every five women over sixteen (42.7%) were in the labor force.

Some landmark dates in the changing status of women are:

1837–Oberlin College admitted women on same basis as men

1887–Susanna Salter elected mayor of Argonia, Kansas

1917–Jeannette Rankin took seat in Congress (only person to vote against two declarations of war)

1918–Annette Adams became first United States Attorney (in California)

1919–American-born Lady Astor elected to British House of Commons

1920–Marie Luhring first woman member of Society of Automotive Engineers

1922–Florence Allen elected to Supreme Court of Ohio; in 1934 became first woman on United States Court of Appeals

1923–Mabel Reineck appointed U.S. Collector of Internal Revenue for Illinois

1931–Jean Wittick budget commissioner of Minnesota
Hattie Caraway elected to United States Senate.

A few cases indicate that the courts, while not by any means classifiable as advocates of Women's Lib, were aware of the changing status of more than half of the population and willing to accept their work outside the home as calling for changes in law. In 1948, for example, Justice Frankfurter spoke for a 6 to 3 majority to uphold a statute that allowed women to be waitresses in taverns but not bartenders. On behalf of the woman who brought the suit, it was contended that the motive was not to protect women from employment in supposedly unsavory places but simply to reserve the better-paid jobs for men.

"The Court does not require legislatures to reflect sociological insight, or shifting social standards, any more than it requires them to keep abreast of the latest scientific standards," Frankfurter wrote, holding that the states were quite free to draw "a sharp line between the sexes."

Changing ideas about the role of women in society seems to have changed the justice's mind. In 1960, he again spoke for the

Court to reject the common-law rule that man and wife are legally one, and that one was the husband. Frankfurter refused to allow the Court "to be obfuscated by medieval views regarding the legal status of women and the common law's reflection of them."

State courts took Frankfurter's 1960 remarks as more applicable to today's world than the rule he announced in 1948. One example was a 1970 New York decision that ended exclusion of women from bars, specifically McSorley's Old Ale House. Another was a New Jersey Supreme Court ruling the same year that the police power no longer could be exercised to forbid women to be bartenders. In this particular instance, a tavern owner was suing for the right to hire a woman against the provisions of an ordinance of Hawthorne Borough. Such decisions recalled for one observer, who had been a speakeasy patron at the onset of Prohibition, the remark of an elderly clubman-about-town who had glared at two young women placidly sipping cocktails at the other end of the bar: "That's what Prohibition has done to this country. It's let women into the bars, and we'll never get them out."

This philosophy, the "male chauvinism" decried by five generations of feminists in this country, had been blatantly behind the Illinois rule that Mrs. Bradwell had complained of in vain and that could still be considered a precedent, although it does not appear to have been cited as such. It was just as blatantly behind a modern Idaho statute that copied older ones in setting the rules for the order in which survivors should be appointed administrators of the property of someone who dies without making a will. The top of the list was the surviving spouse, then the children, then the father or mother, and so on down eleven categories, the last of which was "any person legally qualified." Another passage modified this: "Of several persons claiming and equally entitled to administer, males must be preferred to females, and relatives of the whole to those of the half blood."

In 1967, Sally M. Reed, who was separated from her husband, Cecil, applied to administer the estate of their adopted minor son—property estimated at less than $1,000. Before the date set for a hearing on her application, Cecil Reed filed a petition, too, and the probate court, mentioning the law's specific requirement that males be preferred, issued letters of administration to him. Sally Reed took her case to a state court, which held the law violated the equal protection clause of the Fourteenth Amendment. The state supreme court reversed this judgment in 1970, and the appeal went to Washington. One of the cases cited to prove that the United States Supreme Court had jurisdiction was the miscegenation ruling in *Loving v. Virginia*, described in Chapter 1.

Chief Justice Burger needed little time to deliver the opinion reversing Idaho's supreme court, and overruling *Bradwell v. Illinois* in the process. Half of his time was taken up by his statement of the case, after which he announced:

> Having examined the record and considered the briefs and oral arguments of the parties, we have concluded that the arbitrary preference established in favor of males . . . cannot stand in the face of the Fourteenth Amendment's command that no State deny the equal protection of the laws to any person within its jurisdiction.

While states may treat different classes of people differently, these words "deny to states the power to legislate that different treatment be accorded to persons . . . on the basis of criteria wholly unrelated to the objective of the statute."

The sex of an administrator clearly has no relation to the purpose of this law, which was to get estates administered by someone close to the deceased who was also competent. In arguments before the Court, the theory that men are better qualified than women as administrators was mentioned. The Court was not impressed, for, as the Chief Justice put it, "we can judicially notice that in this country, presumably due to the greater longevity of women, a large proportion of estates both intestate and under wills of decedents, are administered by surviving widows."

The *Reed* case has not ended discrimination against women in our society any more than *Brown* ended discrimination against blacks. But the first step toward righting old wrongs is to get rid of the legal sanction for those wrongs. Whether or not the confrontations between black and white are destined to be repeated between men and women, the Court in this, the last monumental reversal before this book was completed, was a little bit ahead of the public—at least the male public.

Afterword

The preceding chapters are as illustrative of our type of law, in the broadest sense, as they are of the Supreme Court. Law as well as the Court changes, not through the whims of individuals or weak acquiescence to the demands of stronger wills, but through the working of society's evolution.

Mores change at different rates in different cultures, under different forms of government and at differing times. The pace of societal change is by no means a constant in any folkway.

Because the Supreme Court represents law at its best in this country, its response to change is enlightening as well as important. Change often creates a chain reaction. Thus the alterations in the status of women may be a prognosis of change in the legal rights of children. Already some signs of this appear in connection with the claim of right to counsel quite apart from their parents' lawyers for those under certain ages. On another front, the laws of libel and slander, literary property, and privacy are being influenced by instant visual communications from such distances that no one nation or people can control what they will hear and see.

What are we to expect as knowledge and its dissemination increase in the fields of genetics and drugs, the realms of space, the spread of computers, surveillance by satellite, and in electronics? Law as it relates to birth and death, freedom and health, the right to speak and remain silent can be revolutionized through new skills and discoveries. The function of law is to set the rules so that men can be the gainers from scientific advances rather than be enslaved by them.

The very speed with which an idea or an item of news can be circulated at the same time in almost every home in the nation has a direct effect upon the law. In this sense we are becoming more and more a people with a single set of folkways and patterns of behavior. Communication is part of the energy under the melting pot. The instant transmission of communications from every part of the country subjects us to many of the exact same stimuli wherever we live. This means that the rationale for our fifty states as separate experimental legal laboratories will be under increased pressures. Until now one national divorce law was impossible. Would it be modeled on the state statute that restricts grounds for divorce to adultery? Or would we grant the decree on statements of incompatability after a brief notice? As we become more nearly one people, this question loses some of its legal difficulty. Even in divorce, we may now be approaching the point where a national standard to meet the needs of the whole country can soon be developed.

The role of the Supreme Court as well as the legislative

branches is bound to alter, as it has altered throughout its history depending on the extent and pace of communication. At times the Court has been a less accurate reflection of the national will than the elected legislatures. At other times, the Court has offered a better reflection, and at times even taken the lead, since interpretation is not alien to the power to legislate.

A factor of change, if we continue to relate law to the "juices of life" rather than words in buckram volumes, will of course be the variety of ideas that we permit in the marketplace of thought. The shrinking number of the daily press, the consolidation of power in the television and radio fields, the decline in the production of domestic movies narrow the marketplace vis-à-vis a growing population, basically changed by a vast extension of life expectancy from 1787, when forty-two delegates invented in four months our Constitution. But the great First Amendment has a heartening strength in the ten thousand local English-language weeklies that have grown about 40 percent in circulation in the past few years.

A second requirement of flexibility is the need of privacy and secrecy in the earliest stages of the development of new programs. Thus the Founding Fathers at the great Convention of 1787, in the second resolution presented to the gathering, provided in effect that all meetings and discussions should be secret so that the delegates might more readily change their minds. There was not a single leak to our then 100 newspapers during the four months of convention sittings. Purloinment has only recently become a vogue of a few respectable mass media.

Secrecy may well be the essential element for man, so that judge or layman may readily change his early mind. Having once taken a stance it becomes difficult for any mortal to admit a change of mind. Some students trained in sociology and other new sciences might enjoy testing to find a common denominator for those judges who most readily adopted about-faces with the greatest conviction. We would like to know if this facility of about-face has any relationship to the age of the jurist at the time of appointment, his age at the time of change, or approaching retirement. A student in this area of human behavior might start with the ages of the justices at time of appointment to the high bench, length of service at the time of the about-face, and other personal demographic factors. Of course, the law of probabilities will be subject to the great increase of life expectancy since 1787, the fact that appointments to the Supreme Court are for life and that the number of justices on the bench has fluctuated.

Only judges who joyously accept change will recognize that law must keep in step with life. We suspect that this quality will continue to manifest itself on the Supreme Court, and that the Court will change its mind accordingly as circumstances—that is, life or our way of life—dictate. In this sense law is an instrument of change—as is all of life; not too fast, or often, and not too slow. Of course, the setting, the problem, and the challenge depend on the variety of peoples who constitute a nation of law, the territorial size, the measures of literacy, the number of non-communicable languages, and above all the mores pressing for a melting pot or for variety. Such are some of the components of the urge for about-face. Few of the law-literate societies have tried our experiment. Few will not envy our admirable record of about-face.

Index